Aga Roast
Louise Walker

About the author

In 1994, Louise Walker's *The Traditional Aga Cookery Book* was published. It marked the beginning of a remarkable series of titles that have been consistent sellers and a source of inspiration and reassurance for tens of thousands of Aga owners all over the world.

Louise has written seven *Traditional Aga* titles to date. She runs cookery classes from around the four-oven Aga in her home in Bath, and travels to Aga shops all over the United Kingdom to demonstrate to both new and seasoned Aga owners.

Aga Roast is her eleventh book.

Aga Roast

Louise Walker

A. Absolute Press

First published in Great Britain
in 2010 by
Absolute Press
Scarborough House
29 James Street West
Bath BA1 2BT
Phone 44 (0) 1225 316013
Fax 44 (0) 1225 445836
E-mail office@absolutepress.co.uk
Website www.absolutepress.co.uk

This paperback edition first published
in 2013.

Publisher Jon Croft
Commissioning Editor Meg Avent
Art Director Matt Inwood
Design Matt Inwood and
Claire Siggery
Photographer Mike Cooper
Food Styling Genevieve Taylor

ISBN 13: 9781408193471
Printed and bound by C&C Printing

A note about the text
This book was set using Century.
The first Century typeface was cut in
1894. In 1975 an updated family of
Century typefaces was designed by
Tony Stan for ITC.

Bloomsbury Publishing Plc
50 Bedford Square, London
WC1B 3DP
www.bloomsbury.com

Contents

Roasting
in the Aga

One of the best meals to come from an Aga is a roast!

For so many families a roast meal has become a rarity or a meal for a special occasion. For many people meat is now eaten less on a day to day basis than a few years ago so a roast is regarded, rightly, as special.

Roasting meat is often discussed during my cookery demonstrations and a good roast joint will always 'sell' an Aga to a wavering would-be owner. Because a roast meal is so special, often a time for family and friends, it is important to get everything right, without the cook being totally frazzled! In this book I have given a lot of hints and tips that I have garnered over the years to help you produce the prefect roast.

So, first things first: find yourself a good butcher. You cannot hope to serve a good roast meal with poor quality meat. Look for a butcher who is welcoming, where the staff are helpful and can cut the joint to suit your needs. The shop should look and smell clean and the meat on display should look fresh and be well presented. A good butcher will know where his meat comes from and he will probably have cared for and butchered the meat himself. If he sells his meat with pride, you will want to return to his shop often.

A good butcher should have a loyal following and once found you should only buy your meat from that butcher – they all need our support. I travel half an hour out of Bath to buy my meat. It is a small effort to pay for the quality of the meat and the service that I receive from Brian Mitchard. I very rarely buy meat anywhere else.

Aga ROAST

Hanging and butchering

Choosing a good piece of meat is very important whether it be for fast or slow roasting. And what ever joint you buy it will need to be well hung. Hanging allows the flavour to develop and the muscle to tenderise. It also allows the meat to dry out so that there will be less shrinkage during cooking. This reduction in weight does of course cost the butcher and so meat that has been well cared for by a butcher will often cost more than a quickly slaughtered and butchered piece of meat.

Meat for roasting needs to come from parts of the animal where there is little movement, for example the breast meat on birds is more tender than the wing, the sirloin (back) of beef is more tender than the shin. These muscles need less time to tenderise and will roast well. Slow roasting can be more of a compromise where a slightly cheaper cut will become tender with slightly longer cooking, something for which the Aga is perfect.

Meat on the bone has more flavour and cooks more quickly than a rolled joint but boned and rolled joints are popular for easy carving.

Resting

It is essential to give roast meat time to rest – at least 15–20 minutes after removing from the oven and before carving. During cooking the juices from the meat move to the outside of the joint. Resting allows the juices to seep back into the joint which will make carving easier and the meat more tender to eat. This allows time to make the gravy and cook the last minute vegetables.

Remember to add any juices that come from the meat during resting or carving to the gravy for added flavour.

Carving

The idea of carving a joint seems to throw some people into a panic.

It is long been tradition that the man of the house will carve. This of course originated so as to free the cook (the woman!) to do all the final bits and pieces for the meal. For special occasions the meat is often carved at the table with a little ceremony so the carver needs to feel confident.

Before attempting to carve get equipped with some basic good-quality tools.

It is easiest to carve on a wooden board. Choose one that has a channel to catch all the juices. You can also carve on a shallow plate, again easy to carve on but with a shape to catch the juices. I find a non-slip mat under these useful.

You'll also need a carving knife and fork with a steel to sharpen the knife. The forks for carving have long prongs to hold the meat steady and some have finger guards as well. The knives should have a long blade with curved ends. It is useful to have knives of different lengths for different meats and joints. Serrated knives only tear meat and should be avoided.

The most important thing about a knife is its sharpness. Keep it sharpened with a steel or good sharpener and if needed ask your butcher to sharpen the knife periodically.

The aim of carving is to cut slices of meat that will look appetising and be evenly sliced. Carve the meat as thinly as possible and don't scoop out any pieces. Arrange the carved slices neatly on the board or plate.

BEEF

Rolled and boned joints are sliced across the grain.
Slow-cooked joints such as brisket are best sliced at a 45 degree angle.
Fillet cooked individually and sliced into medallions.
Rib of beef on the bone should be chined by your butcher. This loosens the backbone from the ribs. When carving, remove the backbone along with any yellow tendon before carving off the ribs. Loosen some of the meat from the rib bone and carve off the thin slices and then repeat the loosening as you work your way along the joint.

LAMB

Rack of lamb must be chined by the butcher to enable easy carving. Remove the chined bone and then carve down between the ribs so you end up with cutlets.
For leg of lamb, I find this method easier than the usual 'V' cut down to the bone: hold the shank bone that will be exposed slightly from the roasting (use a clean napkin for this). Start on the round side and cut off slices from the shank end parallel to the bone. Turn the leg round as you go.
Loin or saddle. Carve long slices of meat parallel to the back bone. Once cut, slide the knife underneath to release the slices. If they are too long cut each slice in half. Turn the joint over and carve the fillet.
Shoulder. This is a fiddly joint to carve and as a result is often cooked boned. However the meat when cooked on the bone is wonderfully sweet. Hold the joint firmly with a fork and with the thickest part of the joint uppermost. Cut the meat out in a 'V' section in the middle of the joint which will be meaty and without bone. Find this with some probing with the tip of the knife. Carve off slices of meat from the blade bones and the knuckle ends.

VEAL

Veal joints are carved in the same way as lamb.

PORK

Rolled joints. Remove the crackling first; slide the knife underneath it and remove. Cut into strips for serving. Cut thin slices of meat across the grain.
Leg of pork. Cut thin slices down to the bone.
Crown roast. Carve this as you would a rack of lamb.
Loin of pork. Remove the chine bone. Run the knife between the remaining meat and bones and ease off on to a board. Slide the knife under the crackling and remove ready to cut in to strips. Carve the meat in to thin slices
Ham. Hold the ham by the knuckle and carve as for leg of lamb.

DUCK AND GOOSE

Ducks and geese do not have the thick breast meat that you find on a chicken. Cut off the wings and legs and cut the leg into thigh and drumstick through the joints. Holding the bird with the fork, cut the meat from the breast parallel to the bone.

CHICKEN, TURKEY AND PHEASANT

These are very similar and can be carved in the same way. Smaller birds can be cut in half through the breast bone and backbone and served as a half-bird portion.

Place the bird on a board with the breast uppermost. Hold the bird firmly with the fork through the breast bone and cut down between the leg and the body. Push the leg outwards and ease away from the bird, cut through the joint and remove the leg. Set aside and keep warm.

Turn the bird round and put the knife between the wing and the breast and cut through to remove the wing.

Cut the leg and wing from the other side of the bird. For the wings, remove the wing tips and discard. For turkey, slice the meat from the bone of the legs and serve as dark meat. For pheasant and chicken the leg and wing pieces are served as portions.

Next carve the breast. Hold the knife horizontally, parallel to the board. Take a slice through one side of the bird into the lower breast bone just above the leg and wing joints. Slide the knife through to the breast bone. Remove the knife. Now take thin slices from the top of the breast down towards the cut. Thin slices of breast meat will fall away.

Serve a selection of white and dark meats on a serving platter.

Poultry

Chicken is the first meat to which many of us turn; one which is widely available and affordable. Turkey is a much larger bird which appears on our dining tables maybe just once or twice a year. Goose vies for that same festive showpiece spot, and it is on special occasions too that we might choose duck. Here are recipes for them all.

Chicken and Turkey

CHICKEN is far and away the most popular meat eaten in this country. I think there are two reasons for this; it is mass produced (often in unpleasant conditions) and is therefore cheap. It is also a meat that takes a variety of flavours. Some would say chicken needs all these flavours to make the texture and flavour more interesting.

So, to achieve the best results, always try to buy a free-range bird. Yes, it will be more expensive than factory produced birds, but besides giving you a clearer conscience, it will give you a much better flavour, texture and often more meat to the bone than a battery produced hen.

TURKEY is originally an American bird now very popular at Christmas and sometimes at Easter. The birds are often large so are most suitable when catering for a crowd. At other times turkey joints can be used.

Choose your turkey from a reliable source and make sure it has been hung to allow the flavours to develop. It isn't always necessary to be seduced by the 'free-range, organic, blacktail' labels. Rely on a good butcher and a good turkey will be enjoyed. Remember when collecting the bird from the butcher to make a note of the dressed weight, a lot of domestic scales won't be strong enough to weigh a turkey and this known weight is essential to calculate cooking times.

Years of doing Christmas cookery demonstrations have taught me much that helps to take the stress away from the traditional Christmas roast turkey. Indeed, most of these pointers serve as a good guide to cooking roasts in general:

* Relax, this is like any other roast meal – just larger.
* Don't tell anyone what time you plan to serve in case things take a little longer.
* Sit down a few days before with pen and paper and plan a cooking programme.
* Work out the cooking time of the turkey and allow for resting before carving.
* Remember to add the weight of any stuffing to the weight of your bird.
* Whichever method of roasting the turkey in an Aga you use (see page 16), it must have one hour in the roasting oven to get it hot.
* Do not cook straight from the fridge. Have the bird at room temperature for an hour before putting it in the oven.
* See my *Traditional Aga Christmas* book for full details of how to cope with a Christmas meal.

With chicken and turkey it is essential to be hygienic in the kitchen. Both of them are carriers of salmonella and campylobacter, bacteria that cause food poisoning. High heat will kill the bacteria so it is essential that the meat is thoroughly cooked, with no sign of pinkness on the flesh. When storing the raw meat in the fridge keep it low down in the fridge on a plate so that no juices can drip on other food or other foods brush against the raw meat. Always wash hands and utensils thoroughly during and after preparation. Don't wash the meat as this can spray bacteria around the sink area and is unnecessary.

Roasting Chicken in the Aga

Chicken itself is particularly quick to roast because the hollow cavity of the bird allows heat to penetrate during cooking. Untie the legs if roasting without stuffing to allow even roasting.

Stuffing the bird adds flavour, but do remember to add the weight of the stuffing to the weight of the bird to calculate cooking times. I prefer to put an onion or lemon in the cavity for flavour.

Sometimes there is an amount of excess fat in the cavity, I tend to remove that so that any gravy isn't too fatty. If you like gravy with some colour put some slices of onion underneath the chicken. These can be discarded when the chicken is served if you don't need them but the pan juices should give colour to the gravy.

Classic roast chicken

For roasting a chicken a basic guideline is: 20 minutes per 450g/1lb plus 20 minutes.

Put the bird in a roasting tin. If the bird is stuffed remember to add this weight to the total. A little olive oil can be rubbed on the skin if liked.

Hang the roasting tin on the third set of runners from the top of the roasting oven and roast for the calculated time.

Conventional cooking: Roast the chicken in a pre-heated oven at 200C/400F/Gas mark 6.

Test that the bird is cooked (see below) and allow to rest in a warm place for 20 minutes before carving.

To test that chicken, poussin or turkey is cooked, insert a skewer through the thickest part of the thigh in to the breast. Any juices that run should be clear. If they are at all pink return the bird to the oven for at least 20 minutes and then re-test.

I often have difficulty with getting juices to run so insert a sharp knife where the breast and leg join and have a look at the flesh: there should be no sign of pinkness and the leg should move easily.

An increasing number of people like to use a temperature probe to test their birds for doneness. Insert the probe through the thickest part of the bird – avoiding any bone – and through into the cavity. Put an onion in the cavity and use this to anchor the probe. When cooked the probe will reach 80C.

Roasting Turkey in the Aga

Roasting a turkey causes cooks a lot of anxiety, but that can often have more to do with the distraction of family and festivities than any intrinsic difficulty with the bird.

Classic roast turkey

Turkey can be roasted using either the fast, medium or slow methods listed below. Whichever method you choose prepare your turkey in the following way. First, stuff the neck end of the bird. Weigh or work out the total weight. Lattice the top with streaky bacon, if liked. Place the turkey in a large roasting tin. If using bacon put a small piece of foil or a butter paper over the bacon to prevent it browning too much. Hang the roasting tin on the bottom set of runners and roast the turkey for 1 hour. Then choose the method from below which best suits you and continue to roast for the time stated in the chart opposite.

FAST method, leave the turkey in the roasting oven for the entire cooking time.
MEDIUM method, after the first hour in the roasting oven move the turkey to the baking oven of a 3 or 4 oven Aga.
SLOW method, after the first hour in the roasting oven move the turkey to the simmering oven of a 2, 3 or 4 oven Aga.

	FAST 2, 3 and 4 oven Agas	**MEDIUM** 3 and 4 oven Agas	**SLOW** 2, 3 and 4 oven Agas
3.6–5.4kg / 8–12lbs	1¾–2 hours	1½–2½ hours	3–5 hours
5.5–7.25kg / 12–16lbs	2–2½ hours	2½–3½ hours	5–7½ hours
7.25–9kg / 16–20lbs	2½–3 hours	3½–4½ hours	7½–10 hours
9–10.8kg / 20–24lbs	3–3½ hours	4½–5½ hours	10–12½ hours
10.8–12.6kg / 24–28lbs	3½–4 hours	5½–6½ hours	12½–15 hours

Remove the turkey from the oven, check that it is cooked. Lift onto a warm serving platter or carving board and leave to rest for 20–30 minutes before carving. This allows plenty of time for gravy to be made with the pan juices.

Conventional cooking: If you have the choice with your oven cook the bird without the fan. The fan has a tendency to dry out food and when cooking turkey for a long time we are aiming for a moist meat. Alternatively the turkey can be cooked wrapped in foil which will allow the meat to steam cook. Open the foil for the last 30 minutes of cooking to allow the bird to brown.
Pre-heat the oven to 220C/425F/Gas mark 7.
    Put in the turkey and cook for 30–40 minutes before reducing the oven temperature to 170C/325F/Gas mark 3 for the remaining calculated time.

Roasting Goose and Duck in the Aga

Classic roast goose

Goose can be deceptive as it has a heavy carcass and is a large bird that will not always give a lot of meat. I always like to have plenty of stuffing for the goose just in case it is 'family hold back'!

Be sure to cook the goose on a rack so the excess fat can be poured off during cooking. Keep the fat in the fridge ready for roasting potatoes.

A 4.5kg/10lb goose will serve 8 people.

Weigh the stuffed goose, or add the weight of the stuffing to the known weight of the goose.

Calculate the cooking time at 15 minutes per 450g/1lb plus 15 minutes

Stand a rack inside the roasting tin. Prick the skin of the goose all over and rub with salt. Stand the stuffed and trussed goose on the rack and hang the tin on the third set of runners from the top of the roasting oven. As the goose will give up a lot of fat it may be worth pouring off some of the fat half way through the roasting time. As the goose is so fatty there is no need to baste. When the goose has been roasted for the required time it should be golden brown all over. Remove to a warm plate and leave to rest for 20–25 minutes before carving.

Conventional cooking: Start in a pre-heated oven at 220C/200C Fan/425F/Gas mark 7 for half an hour and then reduce the oven to 200C/180C Fan/400F/Gas mark 6.

Classic roast duck

Duck often has to be ordered from the butcher these days as it is difficult to find a whole bird anywhere else. Most of the duck in our shops is sold as portions. Most of it is 'Ayelsbury' duck though most ducks are bred in Norfolk. Try to feel the bird to make sure it has some meat on the breast.

The cavity of the duck can be stuffed but add the weight of the stuffing to the weight of the duck for cooking times.

Stand a rack inside a roasting tin. Prick the skin of the duck all over and rub with salt and a little flour. Stand the duck on the rack and hang the tin on the third set of runners from the top of the roasting oven for 25 minutes per 450g/1lb

Remove the duck from the tin and leave to stand on a warm plate for 10–15 minutes before carving. Pour the fat from the tin and use for roasting potatoes.

Conventional cooking: Roast at 180C/160C Fan/350F/Gas mark 4.

Honey-roast Chicken
with Roast Sweet Potatoes

Roast this all in one dish for a sweet and sticky meal. Serve with a plain green salad to offset the sweetness of the chicken and sweet potatoes.

1.75kg/4lb chicken
1 orange
1 bunch spring onions
110g/4oz honey
3 tablespoons olive oil
½ teaspoon cloves
1 teaspoon paprika

1 teaspoon ground coriander
2 teaspoons cumin
Salt and pepper
1kg/2¼lbs sweet potatoes
1 tablespoon chopped coriander

Serves 6

Line a roasting tin with Bake-O-Glide. Put in the chicken.

Grate the rind from the orange and put in a basin. Finely chop half the bunch of spring onions. Add the honey, oil, cloves, paprika, coriander, cumin and salt and pepper. Use half the mixture to brush the chicken inside and out.

Slice the orange and chop the remaining onion. Use half to put in the chicken cavity and sprinkle the remaining onion over the chicken and the remaining orange slices on the chicken breast.

Hang the tin on the third set of runners from the top of the roasting oven and calculate the roasting time at 20 minutes per 450g/1lb plus 20 minutes.

Meanwhile, peel and cut the sweet potatoes into chunks and toss with the remaining honey mixture. After the first 30 minutes of roasting the chicken add the potatoes round the bird. Remove the orange slices if browning too much.

Roast for the remaining time. The chicken should have a dark golden skin.

Test that the chicken is cooked and then remove the chicken to a warm plate and scatter the coriander over the sweet potatoes.

Serve the sweet potatoes with any pan juices and chunkily carved chicken.

Conventional cooking: Roast at 190C/375F/Gas mark 5.

Cook's note
If your honey has gone thick and crystalline stand it at the back of the Aga to bring it back to a pouring consistency.

Tarragon Chicken

This is a classic chicken dish with lovely aniseed flavours in the flesh and the sauce. Years ago I used to make it with dried tarragon but now fresh tarragon is always available and much nicer. Keep tasting the sauce to avoid overdoing the tarragon flavour.

1.75kg/4lb chicken	or vermouth
1 lemon	300ml/½ pint double cream
4 stalks tarragon	or crème fraîche
50ml/2fl oz dry white wine	Salt and pepper

Cut the lemon in half and use one half to rub the juice all over the chicken skin. Put the squeezed lemon in the cavity of the chicken along with three stalks of the tarragon. Loosely tie the legs together and place the chicken in a small roasting tin.

Hang the tin on the third set of runners from the top of the roasting oven and roast the chicken for 1–1¼ hours (or 20 minutes per 450g/1lb plus 20 minutes if a different weight).

While the chicken is roasting strip the leaves from the remaining stalk of tarragon and chop the leaves. Set aside for the sauce.

When the chicken is cooked remove to a warmed plate and allow to rest while making the sauce.

Skim any excess fat from the roasting tin. Stand the tin on the simmering plate and pour in the wine or vermouth. Bring to the boil while scraping any residues from the tin. The wine will probably reduce to a small amount very quickly. Then pour in the cream or crème fraîche and whisk while it comes to the boil. Allow the sauce to reduce slightly and thicken. Remove from the heat and whisk in 2–3 tablespoons of chopped tarragon, salt and pepper to season and a squeeze of lemon juice. Keep tasting and adjusting to get the balance right.

Carve the chicken and serve with the tarragon sauce and some lightly cooked vegetables.

Conventional cooking: Roast at 190C/375 F/Gas mark 5.

Cook's note
Ensure you use double cream or full-fat crème fraîche otherwise the sauce will 'split' when heating through.

Spicy Roast Chicken

This is a great way to get a spicy flavour into chicken. Serve with chilli roast potatoes or perhaps rice for a change. If you cannot source date and tamarind chutney use a spicy mango chutney instead – though it may not need letting down with water.

2 cinnamon sticks
6 cardamom pods
4 curry leaves
1.6kg/3½lb chicken
1 tablespoon vegetable oil
2 small red fresh chillies, seeded and finely chopped
2 teaspoons grated fresh ginger

2 cloves garlic, peeled and crushed
2 teaspoons ground cumin
2 teaspoons ground coriander
1 teaspoon garam masala
4 tablespoons date and tamarind chutney or hot and spicy mango chutney
1 tablespoon water

Serves 6

Place the cinnamon sticks, cardamom pods and curry leaves in the chicken cavity. Close the cavity and fix together with a cocktail stick or skewer. Tie the legs together and tuck under the wings.

Mix together the oil, chillies, ginger, cumin, coriander and garam masala. Rub this well all over the chicken and stand the chicken in a non-metallic dish. Cover and refrigerate for about an hour.

Place the chicken in a small roasting tin. Hang the tin on the third set of runners from the top of the roasting oven and roast the chicken for 1 hour.

Meanwhile blend the chutney with the water. When the chicken has been cooking for 1 hour remove from the oven and brush it all over with the chutney. Return to the oven for a further 30 minutes until the skin is crispy and golden brown and the chicken is cooked.

Conventional cooking: Roast at 190C/375F/Gas mark 5.

Cook's note
Chunks of potato tossed in oil and a little chopped chilli can be roasted round the chicken. Put the potato round the chicken at the start of cooking.

Roast Summer Chicken

I don't often stuff my roast chickens but for a change I tried this idea to use up some leftover bread and to make the chicken go further. It adds a delicious flavour as well!

2kg/4½lb chicken
2 tablespoons olive oil
1 onion, finely chopped
3 cloves garlic, finely chopped
2 large tomatoes, skinned and chopped

110g/4oz white bread, diced
Salt and pepper
1 tablespoon chopped parsley
1 tablespoon chopped basil
10 green olives, stoned and roughly chopped

Serves 6–8

Remove any excess fat from the cavity of the chicken and put the chicken in a roasting tin.

Prepare the stuffing. Heat the olive oil in a frying pan and sauté the onions until softening. Add the garlic and cook until soft but not brown. Tip into a mixing bowl. Add all the remaining ingredients and stir gently to mix. Use this mixture to stuff the cavity of the chicken. If preparing this chicken some time in advance of cooking ensure that the stuffing is cold before putting in the cavity.

Smear a little olive oil over the chicken and then hang the roasting tin on the third set of runners from the top of the roasting oven for 20 minutes per 450g/1lb plus 20 minutes (remember to add the weight of stuffing to the bird weight). Test to see the chicken is cooked and remove from the oven and allow to rest before carving.

Conventional cooking: Roast at 190C/375F/Gas mark 5.

Cook's note
Serve with new potatoes which you have tossed in harissa paste before roasting.

Thyme-roasted Chicken

Thyme is a good standby herb that adds a lovely dimension to chicken.

2kg/4½lb chicken
2–3 sprigs thyme
50g/2oz butter
2 cloves garlic, peeled and
  chopped

1 tablespoon chopped
  parsley
2 tablespoons chopped
  thyme leaves
Salt and pepper

Serves 6

Remove any excess fat from the cavity of the chicken. Put in the sprigs of thyme and put the chicken in a roasting tin.

Mix together the butter, garlic, parsley, thyme and a grinding of salt and pepper. This can be done in a processor.

Smear the thyme butter over the top of the chicken. If time permits leave the chicken to absorb the flavours for 1–2 hours.

Roast the chicken on the bottom set of runners of the roasting oven for 20 minutes per 450g/1lb plus 20 minutes. Check that the chicken is cooked and allow to rest for 20 minutes before carving.

Conventional cooking: Roast in a pre-heated oven at 190C/375F/Gas mark 5.

Cook's note
Toss some roast new potatoes in homemade pesto made with parsley or watercress.

Roast Goose
with a Potato and Apple Stuffing

Goose is traditionally stuffed with potatoes but I like to add apples as well to add some moisture and tang to offset the richness of the meat.

4.5kg/10lb oven-ready goose
1 tablespoon flour

For the stuffing
1kg/2¼lb hot, mashed potato
1 large onion, peeled and finely chopped
1 large cooking apple,

peeled cored and chopped
Liver from the goose, finely chopped
75g/3oz butter, melted
2 tablespoons chopped parsley
Salt and pepper
1 egg, beaten

Serves 8

Wipe the goose outside and in, removing any giblets. Chop the liver.

Mix together all the stuffing ingredients, binding together with the beaten egg. Stuff the tail end of the goose and close the cavity with a skewer or cocktail sticks.

Rub the skin of the goose with the flour and stand on a rack in the roasting tin. Prick the breast of the goose well with a fork.

Hang the tin on the third set of runners from the top of the roasting oven for 20 minutes per 450g/1lb plus 20 minutes. Periodically pour off any fat in the roasting tin.

If the goose is browning too much either move to a lower runner or slide a loose piece of foil over the breast.

Remove the goose from the oven and allow to rest for 15–20 minutes before carving and serving with apple sauce and thin gravy.

Conventional cooking: Put the goose in the oven pre-heated to 220C/ 425F/ Gas mark 7. After the first half-hour turn the oven down to 200C/400F/Gas mark 6.

Cook's note
Reserve the fat for roasting potatoes and parsnips, it will keep for months in the fridge.

Roast Pesto Poussins

Poussin are readily available in the supermarkets and at some butchers. They look attractive individually served but they do need help to bring out flavour. Here some homemade pesto is slipped under the breast skin to add flavour and keep the meat moist.

4 poussin
1 tablespoon olive oil

For the Pesto
110g/4oz pine nuts
2 cloves garlic, peeled and
*   roughly chopped*

Good bunch basil
4 tablespoons olive oil
50g/2oz Parmesan cheese,
*   finely grated*
Salt

Serves 4

Put the pine nuts in a dry frying pan and place on the simmering plate to toast until golden brown – this can be done in the roasting oven, but watch that they don't burn!

Put the pine nuts, garlic, basil leaves stripped from their stalks and most of the oil in a blender or processor. Whizz, gradually adding the remaining oil and the Parmesan. Grind in a seasoning of salt.

Very carefully lift the skin on the breasts of the poussin, taking care not to tear it. Spread a tablespoon of pesto between the skin and the breast meat. Spread any remaining pesto in the cavities of the poussin. Stand the poussin in a roasting tin and rub over the 1 tablespoon of olive oil.

Hang the roasting tin on the third set of runners from the top of the roasting oven and roast the poussin for 40 minutes. Allow to rest for 5 minutes before serving.

Good served with either Italian bread or roast new potatoes.

Conventional cooking: Roast at 180C/350F/Gas mark 4.

Cook's note
This pesto can be made and used in the same way for a chicken if you prefer.
The breast slices will have an attractive green sliver under the skin.

Roast Duck
with a Redcurrant Glaze

Duck lends itself to a fruit accompaniment to counteract the fat. This recipe gives the bird an attractive glaze as well as fabulous flavour.

2.25kg/5lb duckling
125g/5oz redcurrant jelly
1 orange, finely grated zest and the squeezed juice
1 tablespoon juniper berries, crushed

1 clove garlic, peeled and crushed
Salt and pepper
1 orange cut into eighths and fresh redcurrants (if in season) to garnish

Serves 3–4

Remove any giblets from the duck plus any solid visible fat. Prick the duck all over with a fork and put into a roasting tin on the rack on its lowest setting. Hang the tin on the third set of runners from the top of the roasting oven and roast the duck for 20 minutes per 450g/1lb plus 20 minutes. Part way through roasting pour off any excess fat from the tin and use for roasting potatoes.

Meanwhile put the redcurrant jelly, the zest and juice of the orange, the crushed juniper berries and garlic in a basin. Mix well, season and stand at the back of the Aga.

20 minutes before the end of the roasting time, spoon half the glaze over the duck and return to the oven.

When the duck is cooked lift on to a warmed plate to rest. Pour any excess fat from the roasting tin and then pour in the remaining glaze. Stand on the simmering plate and stir for 1–2 minutes then pour over the duck before serving.

Garnish with the oranges and redcurrants.

Conventional cooking: Pre-heat the oven to 200C/400F/Gas mark 6 and roast as above.

Cook's note
If preferred, add a little wine to the glaze in the roasting pan and serve as a sauce rather than a glaze.

Meat

The dark meats – pork, beef
and lamb – offer some of the
most superlative roasts available.
Here I show you how to get the
most from this most wonderful
choice of meats.

Roasting Pork in the Aga

PORK in this country, we seem to forever be told, is under threat. Why? As a nation we have become content to import intensively reared, tasteless, cheap meat. Try a piece of properly reared and butchered British pork and you won't go back to the imported variety.

To my mind nothing beats a roast pork joint with crispy crackling and apple sauce. Even as a cold meat it will be moist and not at all stringy. It should go without saying: always buy pork from a good butcher. The flesh of a good pork joint should look a healthy pale pink, not dark. It will have a generous layer of fat that is firm and white. The skin should be dry and firm.

The fat makes the joint succulent and though fat from meat is no longer fashionable it is essential for flavour and moistness.

I was brought up to eat pork only when there was an 'R' in the month. These days, with careful breeding and handling, pork can safely be eaten all year round.

Sometimes you will be offered meat from traditional breeds such as Gloucester Old Spot or Tamworth. These have a particular flavour and are often much prized, but again look for meat that has been carefully produced and you will be in for a treat.

Pork must always be thoroughly cooked and not at all pink. To test that it is cooked, a skewer inserted into the thickest part will come out hot and all the juices must be clear.

Most pork joints can be roasted. Some joints are very large and need dividing. Some joints roast well boned out and some such as belly benefit from slow roasting to allow all the fat to moisten the meat and allow it to become meltingly tender.

Classic roast loin of pork

Cut a lemon in half and rub the scored skin of the pork with the lemon halves, squeezing over the juice as you go.

Stand the loin of pork in a roasting tin, skin side uppermost.

Hang the tin on the third set of runners from the top of the roasting oven and roast the joint for 30 minutes per 450g/ 1lb plus 30 minutes.

Remove the joint from the oven and stand on a warm plate while making the gravy. Do not cover the joint or put it in the simmering or plate warming oven as this will make the crackling go soft.

To my mind, roast pork has to have good crispy crackling. This is my foolproof method: Ask your butcher to score the skin on the joint really well. Should you or he forget you can use a Stanley knife (carefully) to score the skin yourself. When you get the joint home uncover the skin if wrapped in any form of plastic. Chill. When ready to prepare the joint cut a fresh lemon in half and rub the scored skin well with a lemon half, squeezing on the juice as you go.

Place the meat in the oven and roast. Do not add any salt or oil. You will have perfect crackling after $1-1\frac{1}{2}$ hours in the roasting oven.

Chinese Roast Pork

Pork is used a great deal in Chinese cooking but not often roasted. I like to cook this slowly for several hours in the simmering oven after the first hour in the roasting oven and when all the marinade has been brushed on.

1kg/2¼lbs boneless pork
   shoulder

For the marinade
35g/1½oz ginger, peeled
   and finely chopped
10 cloves garlic, peeled and
   finely chopped

3 tablespoons soft brown
   sugar
2 tablespoons malt vinegar
2 tablespoons soy sauce
350g/12oz honey
250ml/9fl oz Chinese
   cooking wine
2 teaspoons Chinese five-
   spice powder
2 teaspoons sesame oil

Serves 4–6

Mix all the marinade ingredients together in a bowl and add the pork. Rub all the marinade into the pork, cover and refrigerate overnight.

Put a sheet of Bake-O-Glide in the base of the roasting tin and put in the drained joint of pork. Hang the roasting tin on the third set of runners from the top of the roasting oven and roast the meat for 30 minutes.

Meanwhile pour the marinade into a saucepan and stand on the simmering plate. Allow to bubble until reduced and thick.

Remove the pork from the oven and baste well with the marinade mixture. Roast for a further 30 minutes. Baste again. This time put the pork in the simmering oven for 2–3 hours, until cooked through and tender.

Remove the meat from the oven and allow to rest somewhere warm for 15 minutes.

Carve slices of meat and serve with rice and stir-fried vegetables.

Cook's note
Allow the joint to come to room temperature before cooking if it has been marinating in the fridge overnight.

Conventional cooking: Start the joint in a pre-heated oven at 220C/425F/ Gas mark 7. After the first hour turn the oven down to 170C/325F/Gas mark 3 and cook for the remaining time.

Fruity Stuffed Fillet of Pork

Pork and fruit always seems a winning combination. A fillet of pork has a tendency to be dry and is always in danger of being over-cooked so adding a stuffing not only keeps the meat moist but helps it to go further.

1 pork fillet, approx
   450g/1lb
2 tablespoons olive oil
1 small red onion, peeled
   and finely chopped
1 dessert apple, cored and
   finely chopped
75g/3oz ready-to-eat
   apricots, finely chopped
1 tablespoon finely chopped
   sage leaves

Salt and pepper
6 slices Parma ham

For the sauce
150ml/¼ pint dry white
   wine
150ml/¼ pint single cream
2 tablespoons wholegrain
   mustard
Salt and pepper

Serves 4

Prepare the pork fillet by laying on a chopping board. Cut the fillet lengthways, but not cutting all the way through. Open out the fillet like a book. Lay the fillet between two pieces of cling film and bat out with a rolling pin until thin and an even thickness all over.

Prepare the stuffing. Heat the olive oil in a frying pan and add the chopped onion. Sauté until softening but not browning and then add the apple, apricots and sage. Season with salt and pepper and stir well to coat in the oil. Cook gently for 10 minutes, stirring occasionally. Remove from the heat and cool slightly.

Remove the cling film from the meat. Spoon the stuffing down the middle of the pork fillet and bring the sides together.

Lay the prosciutto on a board and put the stuffed loin on top. Wrap the ham round the fillet, but not too tightly otherwise the filling may burst out.

Line a baking tray with Bake-O-Glide and put on the wrapped fillet.

Hang the tray on the third set of runners from the top of the roasting oven and roast the fillet for 30–40 minutes, until crispy on the outside.

Meanwhile make the sauce. Pour the wine into the pan the fruit was cooked in and stand on the simmering plate. Gently stir in the cream and the mustard. Bubble gently and season just before serving with slices of pork fillet.

Conventional cooking: Pre-heat the oven and roast at 200C/400F/Gas mark 6.

Cook's note
Roasting the fillet on a shallow baking tray allows the ham to become crisp. If you only have a deep tin, you may need to cook the fillet on a higher setting.

Paprika Roast Pork

For those who aren't too keen on crackling (there must be some out there...) this recipe tops the joint with bacon and lemon for a change and has a tasty stuffing mix to go with it.

1.25kg/2lb 12oz piece boned and rolled pork shoulder or leg, rind removed
6 rashers streaky bacon
2 cloves garlic, peeled and slivered
1 lemon
3 or 4 sprigs thyme
2 level teaspoons paprika

For the stuffing
4 rashers back bacon, finely chopped
1 clove garlic, peeled and crushed
50g/2oz mushrooms, finely diced
110g/4oz fresh breadcrumbs
2 tablespoons chopped thyme leaves
50g/2oz blue Stilton, crumbled

Serves 6–8

Grate the rind from half the lemon and cut three slices from the lemon. Squeeze the juice from the remaining lemon and set all aside.

Cut slits in the pork and insert the garlic slivers. Weigh the joint and calculate the cooking time; 35 minutes per 450g/1lb plus 35 minutes.

Place the pork in a small roasting tin. In a basin mix together the reserved lemon juice and paprika and smear over the pork joint fat. Lay over the rashers of streaky bacon and slide the lemon slices and sprigs of thyme between them.

Hang the roasting tin on the third set of runners from the top of the roasting oven and roast for the required time. If the bacon becomes too brown slide a loose piece of foil over the top.

Meanwhile prepare the stuffing. Put the bacon in a frying pan and stand on the simmering plate to dry-fry the bacon. Cook for 3–4 minutes then stir in the mushrooms. Cook for 1–2 minutes then add the breadcrumbs, thyme, Stilton and the reserved lemon rind. Stir to mix well. Shape into 6–8 stuffing balls.

Put the stuffing either on a tray lined with Bake-O-Glide or round the joint. Bake for the last 20 minutes of roasting time.

Allow to rest on a warm platter for 10 minutes before carving. Make a gravy from the pan juices and scrapings.

Conventional cooking: Roast the pork at 190C/375F/Gas mark 5.

Cook's note
Add some onion and lemon slices to the potatoes when roasting them for extra levels of flavour.

Slow Roast Belly of Pork

Though belly pork is a cheaper cut it is packed full of flavour. Cooked slowly like this it is meltingly soft and flavoursome.

2 stalks sage, leaves removed and stalks discarded
1 sprig rosemary, leaves removed and stalks discarded
3 cloves garlic, roughly chopped

grated zest and juice 2 lemons
1 kilo/2^1/$_4$lbs boned belly pork
^{1}/$_2$ extra lemon

Serves 4–6

Put the sage and rosemary leaves, the lemon rind and juice and the garlic in a blender and chop as finely as possible. Season with salt and pepper.

Lay the meat flat on a board, skin side down. Make some incisions in the meat and rub over the lemon and herb mixture, taking care not to get the mixture on the skin. If time allows, leave the meat to rest like this for an hour or two.

Put the rack inside the small roasting tin and lay on the meat, skin side uppermost. Squeeze over the juice from the ^{1}/$_2$ lemon, rubbing it in to the skin as you do so.

Hang the roasting tin on the third set of runners from the top of the roasting oven for 50–60 minutes by which time the skin should be crisp. Move the pork joint to the simmering oven and cook for 2–3 hours. The meat should be well cooked and any juices running clear.

Allow the meat to rest for 10–15 minutes before carving into slices.

Serve with apple sauce and a seasonal green vegetable.

Conventional cooking: For the first hour cook the pork in a pre-heated oven at 220C/425F/Gas mark 7. After that hour turn the oven down to 150C/300F/Gas mark 2 for the remaining 2–3 hours.

Cook's notes
Make sure a good crackling has formed before moving the meat to the simmering oven. If your Aga doesn't seem too hot then hang the tin on the second set of runners to get a crispy crackling.

'Barbecued' Spare Ribs

These spare ribs are often associated with barbecues but in this case the term refers more to the type and flavour of the ribs. They make wonderful finger food but be sure to have damp finger wipes to hand!

12–16 meaty Chinese-style spare ribs
2 cloves garlic, peeled
A large cube fresh ginger, peeled
2 tablespoons hoisin sauce
4 tablespoons light soy sauce
Juice 1 small orange

2 tomatoes, skinned, seeded and finely chopped
2 tablespoons rice wine or dry sherry
1 star-anise, crushed
Pinch caster sugar
Ground black pepper
1 tablespoon honey, placed in a basin on the back of the Aga to soften

Serves 4

Trim the bones and separate if needed. Lay in a single layer in a shallow dish. Chop the garlic and ginger finely and rub into the ribs.

Place the hoisin sauce, soy sauce, orange juice, chopped tomatoes, rice wine or sherry, crushed star anise, sugar and a grinding of pepper in a saucepan and bring to the boil, stirring. Remove from the heat and allow to cool. When cool pour over the ribs and make sure they are coated. Cover and refrigerate overnight.

Line a baking tray with a sheet of Bake-O-Glide and lay on the marinated ribs. Hang the tin on the third set of runners from the top of the roasting oven for 20 minutes. Turn the ribs over and cook for another 15 minutes. Remove the ribs from the oven and brush well with the softened honey. Return to the oven for a further 10 minutes until the ribs are a rich golden colour.

Conventional cooking: Roast the spare ribs at 200C/400F/Gas mark 6.

Cook's note
Be sure to line the baking tray with Bake-O-Glide otherwise you will spend hours trying to get the baked-on marinade off your tin!

Roasting Gammon in the Aga

GAMMON, either roasted or boiled is delicious not only hot but useful also for cold cuts. Traditionally cooked at Christmas many only think of it at that time of year and settle for 'plastic' pre-packed ham the rest of the year round. It is so easy to cook that it really should be part of your regular repertoire.

As with all meat find a good butcher. There are still some butchers who cure their own gammons and bacon. Ask if the joint needs soaking before cooking, though these days the gammons are not usually very salty.

You can buy the joint on the bone but it may be a good idea to give the butcher notice of this as usually joints come boned and rolled. Look for a covering of fat and fresh looking meat. If advised, soak the joint in plenty of cold water overnight, changing it at least once.

The joint can be 'boiled' for most of the cooking time and then glazed and finished or roasted wrapped in foil. Both methods are given below.

Boiled ham

This doesn't sound as appetizing as roast ham but the meat is a little more tender and moist cooked this way.

Put a trivet, an old saucer or a good wad of kitchen paper in the base of a large saucepan, sufficient to hold the joint. Stand in the gammon joint. Pour on enough liquid to come no more than 5cm/2 inches up the side of the pan. You can use water, beer, cider or apple juice. I do not like my joints covered in water as the meat becomes too wet during cooking and looses flavour and texture. If you like you can add peppercorns and bay leaves. Cover with a lid.

Stand the pan on the simmering plate for 30 minutes. This allows some heat to get into the joint. After 30 minutes move the pan to the simmering oven and cook for 20 minutes per 450g/1lb.

For conventional cooking simmer very gently on the hob, checking the level of water in the pan in case it dries out.

Remove the joint from the saucepan and drain. Stand on a baking tray lined with Bake-O-Glide and remove the skin. Cut the fat into a diamond pattern and glaze. Hang the baking tray on the bottom set of runners of the roasting oven and allow the meat to glaze for 15–30 minutes.

To glaze the ham pre-heat the oven to 190C/375F/Gas mark 5.

Rest the joint for at least 15 minutes before carving.

Classic roast ham

Soak the joint if needed.

Put the rack on the lowest setting in the roasting tin and stand the meat on it, skin side uppermost. Cover the joint closely with foil and slide the tin onto the bottom set of runners of the roasting oven.

For a conventional oven; cook at 190C/375F/Gas mark 5.

Calculate the cooking time as: 30 minutes per 450g/1lb plus 30 minutes.

Thirty minutes before the end of the cooking time remove the foil and peel off the skin. The skin should peel off easily if the joint is cooked. Cut the fat into a diamond pattern and glaze the joint with your chosen glaze. Return to the roasting oven for the remaining 30 minutes. Rest for at least 15 minutes before carving.

Large gammon joints on the bone

Sometimes you may like to buy a larger joint on the bone and then usually you don't have a saucepan large enough to cook it in. This is the easiest way I know, a combination of roasting and 'boiling'.

Put the rack into the large roasting tin on the lowest setting. Lay the joint on top. Pour in enough liquid to come just to the level of the meat. Add any flavourings and cover the meat tightly with foil. Remember the foil will snag if the tin is hung on the runners so allow for that.

Put the tin on the floor of the roasting oven and cook for 1 hour. Move to the simmering oven and cook the joint for 20 minutes per 450g/1lb. Remove the joint from the oven, peel off the foil and then the skin. Cut the fat into diamonds and add the glaze. Return the pan to the bottom set of runners of the roasting oven for 15–30 minutes until glazed.

Rest the joint for 15 minutes before carving.

With all hams keep wrapped in greaseproof paper or parchment in the fridge. Foil or cling film seems to make the meat sweat and the glaze run.

Glazes for ham and gammon joints

Here are some ideas for glazing your ham joints.

After the initial cooking strip the skin from the joint and cut the fat into diamonds. Stand the joint, fat side uppermost, on a baking tray lined with Bake-O-Glide. Spread on the chosen glaze and finish off in the roasting oven or a pre-heated oven set at 170C/325F/Gas mark 3. Glazing usually takes 15–20 minutes, but keep an eye on it as with the high sugar content it can burn easily.

Maple syrup glaze

Mix together the grated rind of an orange with 3 teaspoons of smooth mustard and 4 tablespoons of maple syrup and spread over the fat. Glaze as above.

Marmalade glaze

Mix together 3 tablespoons of dark Oxford marmalade with 2 teaspoons of smooth mustard and spread over the fat. Glaze as above.

Balsamic glaze

Mix together 4 tablespoons of balsamic vinegar with 3 tablespoons of soft brown sugar and a good grinding of black pepper and spread over the fat. Glaze as above.

Honey glaze

Mix together 2 tablespoons of clear honey with 2 tablespoons of soft brown sugar and 1 teaspoon of English mustard and spread over the fat. Glaze as above.

Rum- and Ginger-glazed Gammon

Any recipe that uses ginger is sure to be a winner with me. This glaze for ham is deliciously warming in winter and makes a change to the usual mustard and sugar glaze.

2.75kg/7lb boneless joint of gammon, smoked or unsmoked

For the glaze
2 tablespoons rum

10 balls crystallised stem ginger
Finely grated zest and juice 1 orange
75g/3oz dark soft brown sugar

Serves 12

Put a trivet or saucer in the base of a large saucepan or casserole and put in the joint of gammon. Add enough water to come just 4cm/1$\frac{1}{2}$ inches up the side of the saucepan. Put on the lid and stand the pan on the simmering plate and slowly bring the gammon to the boil. Allow to simmer for 30 minutes and then move the gammon to the simmering oven for 2$\frac{1}{2}$ hours.

While the gammon is cooking make the ginger glaze. Place the orange juice and rind in a blender or processor and add the rum, ginger and brown sugar. Process until the ginger is well chopped, this may take a minute or two. Pour into a basin until needed.

Remove the pan from the oven and the meat from the pan. Allow to cool slightly before stripping off the skin, leaving a layer of fat. Stand the joint on a tray lined with Bake-O-Glide, fat side uppermost. Score the fat into a diamond pattern. Spoon on the glaze making sure to push it well into the scored fat.

Hang the tray on the third set of runners of the roasting oven for 15 minutes. Check the joint and if it is becoming blackened move the tray lower. You are aiming for a rich, golden glaze. Roast for a further 10–15 minutes.

Remove from the oven and allow to stand for 10–15 minutes before carving if serving hot.

Conventional cooking: Simmer the gammon joint on a low heat on the hob. When glazing put into a pre-heated oven at 190C/375F/Gas mark 5 for 15–20 minutes until glazed and golden brown.

Cook's note
This recipe is enough for 12 but can easily be halved for a smaller joint. The joint will of course need a shorter cooking time but the glazing will take the same time.

Gammon with Spiced Pears

Lightly spiced fruit is always good with gammon. The pears can be prepared a day or two in advance and kept covered in the fridge. Serve at room temperature for full flavour.

For the pears and syrup
1kg/2¹/₄lbs small firm pears
200g/7oz caster sugar
1 cinnamon stick
2 bay leaves and 2 cloves
2 peppercorns
Strip orange rind
2 tablespoons cider vinegar

Piece gammon joint,
*   smoked or unsmoked,*
*   about 1.8kg/4lbs*
2 tablespoons mustard
2 tablespoons soft brown
*   sugar*
Cloves, about 10–12

Serves 6–8

Prepare the syrup. Pour 300ml/¹/₂ pint water into a wide shallow saucepan and add all the remaining ingredients except the pears. Stand the pan on the simmering plate and stir to dissolve the sugar. Bring to the boil and remove from the heat.

Prepare the pears. Try to keep the pears whole if they are very small, alternatively cut each one in half. Peel the pears, keeping the stalk in tact if possible. As each pear is prepared slip it into the syrup. When all the pears are in the syrup cover the pan with a lid, gently bring to the boil and move the pan to the simmering oven. Cook the pears for 20 minutes and test to see if they are just cooked. Test with a skewer. They need to be firm to hold their shape.

Spoon the pears into a bowl and pour over the syrup. Cover and cool.

Put a trivet or old saucer in the base of a deep saucepan. Put in the gammon and pour in enough water to come 4cm/1¹/₂ inches up the side of the pan. Cover with a lid. Stand the pan on the simmering plate and bring the water to the boil. Simmer for 30 minutes and then move the pan to the simmering oven. Cook for 1¹/₂–2 hours.

Remove the pan from the oven and take the joint from the pan. Cool slightly and then remove the skin. Cut a diamond pattern through the fat. Stand the joint, fat uppermost, on a baking tray lined with Bake-O-Glide. Smear the fat with mustard and then press on the sugar. Stud the diamonds with cloves.

Hang the tray of gammon on the bottom set of runners of the roasting oven for 25–30 minutes or until bubbling and golden brown. Allow the meat to stand on a warm plate for 10–15 minutes before carving and serving with the spiced pears.

Conventional cooking: Steam the ham on the hob at a very low temperature for the appropriate cooking time. Glaze the ham and put in a pre-heated oven at 190C/375F/Gas mark 5 to finish.

Cook's note
Ask your butcher if the gammon will need soaking to remove salt before cooking.

Roasting Lamb in the Aga

LAMB is often chosen as the meat for Easter, but whilst strongly associated with this time of year, lambs bred for and sold at Easter are often too young and small and slightly lacking in flavour. However, properly butchered the meat will be meltingly soft. The best lamb is eaten from mid-summer onwards. Lamb above one year in age is classed as mutton, though sometimes difficult to source the added flavour is worth the effort.

Depending upon the age of the lamb it will vary from pale pink to brownish pink, but the flesh must always be clear of blood spots. The fat should be white and brittle, and not too much of it.

Mutton will have a darker flesh but the fat should still be white, avoid if grey or yellow.

Salt-marsh lamb comes from animals that graze on salt-marshes, mainly in Wales or Romney Marshes, although it is now produced all round our island. This lamb is prized for its sweetness and flavour. The animals feed on salty herbs which gives the meat a distinctive, delicate flavour. As this meat is of limited supply expect to pay a premium price for it. Roast in the same way as other lamb.

Being a young animal most joints of lamb can be roasted, the exception being middle neck or scrag-end. These are best cooked slowly.

Classic roast leg of lamb

Roast leg of lamb is often studded with slivers of garlic and rosemary. You can use them together, individually or not at all.

Cut small slits all over the joint of lamb using the point of a sharp knife. Peel two cloves of garlic and cut them into slivers. Break small florets off a twig of rosemary. Slip the slivers of garlic and the florets of rosemary into the slits.

Place the leg of lamb into a roasting tin and grind over a little pepper.

Hang the tin on the third set of runners from the top of the roasting oven and roast for the following time:

Pink: 15 minutes per 450g/1lb plus 15 minutes
Well done: 20 minutes per 450g/1lb plus 20 minutes

Remove from the oven. If you want to check that the lamb is cooked to your requirements a sharp knife inserted in the middle of the joint to the bone should tell you how well the meat is cooked. Put the meat on a warm plate and leave to rest for 10–15 minutes before carving.

Conventional cooking: Roast the lamb in a pre-heated oven at 200C/400F/Gas mark 6.

Moroccan-style Lamb

A roast meal all in one dish easy enough for an everyday meal, packed with flavour.

A boneless half shoulder of lamb, about 1–1¼kg/ 2–3lb in weight
1 clove garlic, peeled and crushed
1 tablespoon ground cinnamon
3 tablespoons olive oil
700g/1½lbs potatoes, peeled and halved and possibly quartered, depending upon size
1 aubergine, cut into 2.5cm/1 inch cubes
200ml/7fl oz dry white wine
110g/4oz ready-to-eat dried apricots
1 tablespoon tomato purée
25g/1oz pine nuts, toasted

Serves 4

In a small bowl mix together the garlic, cinnamon and 1 tablespoon of olive oil. Rub this mixture all over the surface of the joint. Stand the meat in the roasting tin. Hang the tin on the third set of runners from the top of the roasting oven and time for 20 minutes for 450g/1lb plus 20 minutes.

Put the potatoes and aubergines in a bowl and pour on 2 tablespoons of olive oil. Mix well to coat.

1 hour before the end of the calculated cooking time tip the potatoes and aubergines around the meat. Return to the oven for the rest of the cooking time.

Pour the wine into a small saucepan with the apricots, bring to the boil and remove from the heat. Leave to infuse until the meat is cooked.

When the meat and vegetables are cooked lift them from the tin onto a warm plate to rest for 10 minutes before carving.

Strain the wine into the roasting tin and blend it with any cooking juices. Stand the tin on the simmering plate and whisk in the tomato purée.

Serve the meat with the potatoes and aubergines and accompany with the apricots and pine nuts.

Conventional cooking: Pre-heat the oven to 190C/375F/Gas mark 5 and roast as above.

Cook's note
Keep an eye on the cinnamon crust if your Aga is 'hot'. If it is colouring too much then slide a loose piece of foil over it when the potatoes are added.

Roast Lamb
with Summer Vegetables and Mint Pesto

This is certainly not a traditional roast lamb recipe. Here I am using the idea of roasting summer vegetables but adding tender pieces of lamb with them so that we have a complete meal in a dish. Tender pieces of lamb are essential.

700g/1¼lbs lean lamb neck
  fillet or boneless shoulder
  steaks, cubed
450g/1lb new potatoes,
  quartered
3 cloves garlic, peeled and
  crushed
2 small aubergines, topped
  and tailed and cut into
  chunks
2 red peppers, seeded and
  cut into chunks

4 tablespoons olive oil
Salt and pepper

For the pesto
6 tablespoons toasted flaked
  almonds
A good bunch of mint,
  leaves removed and
  stalks discarded
2 teaspoons Dijon mustard
4 tablespoons olive oil

Serves 4

Put the potatoes in a saucepan with 2.5cm/1 inch water and bring to the boil. Drain the water away, cover with a lid and put in the simmering oven for 10 minutes.

In a roasting tin or shallow oven-proof dish put the lamb cubes, potatoes, garlic, aubergine, peppers and oil. Season lightly, toss in the oil and spread out in the dish.

Hang the tin or the shelf if using, on the third set of runners from the top of the roasting oven. Put in the dish of lamb. Roast the meat and vegetables for 45 minutes, until the meat is tender and the vegetables cooked.

While the meat is cooking prepare the pesto. Put the almonds, mint, mustard and seasoning in a blender and whiz to a rough paste. Keep the blender running and slowly pour in the olive oil. Adjust the seasoning. Spoon into a bowl and serve with the roast lamb and vegetables.

Conventional cooking: Pre-heat the oven and roast at 190C/375F/Gas Mark 5

Cook's note
Add different vegetables if you like, such as red onions or courgettes.

Basil and Garlic Roast Lamb

Tomatoes, garlic and basil taste so good with lamb and evoke the flavour of summer at any time of year.

A boned shoulder of lamb
110g/4oz semi-dried
*   tomatoes*
good handful basil leaves
6 cloves garlic, peeled and
*   finely chopped*

110g/4oz fresh
*   breadcrumbs*
4 tablespoons olive oil
salt and pepper
6 tomatoes, halved
*   lengthways*

Serves 6

Put the semi-dried tomatoes, two thirds of the basil leaves, 4 cloves garlic, breadcrumbs, 2 tablespoons olive oil and a seasoning of salt and pepper in a blender or processor and whiz until the tomatoes are finely chopped.

Unroll the boned shoulder and spread over the tomato stuffing. Roll the lamb shoulder and secure in place either with skewers or string. Place the lamb in a roasting tin and hang on the second set of runners from the bottom of the roasting oven. Roast the lamb for 25 minutes per 450g/1lb plus 25 minutes.

When the lamb is cooked remove from the oven and keep warm. Allow the meat to rest while cooking the tomatoes.

Line a small baking tray with Bake-O-Glide and lay on the tomatoes, cut side uppermost. Shred the remaining basil. Drizzle the 2 tablespoons of oil over the tomatoes and sprinkle over the basil and garlic. Hang the tin of cook for 15 minutes, until just tingeing with colour and soft.

Carve the lamb and serve with the tomatoes.

Conventional cooking: Roast this joint in a pre-heated oven at 190C/375F/ Gas mark 5.

Cook's notes
Watery out of season tomatoes may take some time to colour so if you cook this in the winter allow more cooking time if you like your tomatoes a little charred.

Quince-glazed Leg of Lamb

Some of you lucky enough to have a quince tree in your garden may make quince paste or cheese at home, alternatively it is usually available on a good cheese counter or speciality section as 'membrillo'.

1 leg of lamb	2 teaspoons Dijon mustard
50ml/2fl oz orange juice	2 teaspoons olive oil
2 tablespoons quince paste	Salt and pepper

Weigh the lamb and calculate the cooking time at 20 minutes per 450g/1lb plus 20 minutes.

Put the lamb in the roasting tin and hang the tin from the second set of runners from the top of the roasting oven and roast for half the calculated roasting time.

Meanwhile make the glaze. Put all the remaining ingredients in a small saucepan, stand on the simmering plate. Stir over the gentle heat until the quince paste has melted and then allow the glaze to simmer for 2–3 minutes. Remove from the heat.

After half the roasting time, brush some glaze over the lamb and return to the oven. Repeat this every 10 minutes or so.

When the lamb is cooked remove from the oven and brush with any remaining glaze. Leave to rest for 15–20 minutes before carving.

Serve with roast potatoes.

Conventional cooking: Roast at 200C/400F/Gas mark 6. If browning too quickly reduce the temperature to 180C/350F/Gas mark 4.

Cook's note
If the glaze is browning too quickly move the tin to the bottom set of runners of the roasting oven.

Thyme-crusted Leg of Lamb

Cook this in the summer cut into warm chunks with a salad. Perfect for eating in the garden.

1.3kg/3lb butterflied leg of lamb

For the thyme rub
1 clove garlic, peeled and finely chopped
1 tablespoon sunflower oil
Finely grated zest 2 lemons
2 tablespoons chopped thyme leaves
2 teaspoons ground allspice

For the potato and bean salad
200g/7oz cherry tomatoes
1kg/2¹/₄lbs salad potatoes, cooked and quartered if large
250g/9oz green beans, topped, tailed and lightly cooked
Juice ¹/₂ lemon
4 tablespoons extra virgin olive oil
1–2 tablespoons chopped parsley
Salt and pepper

Serves 4–6

In a basin mix together all the thyme rub ingredients. Place the lamb on a board, skin-side uppermost. Make a few slits over the surface and smear over the thyme rub.

Stand a rack in the roasting tin on the highest setting and lay the lamb on top. Hang the roasting tin on the third set of runners from the top of the roasting oven and roast the lamb for 55–60 minutes. Remove from the oven and allow to rest for 10–15 minutes before slicing and serving with the salad.

While the lamb is roasting combine the tomatoes, potatoes and beans in a bowl. Whisk together the lemon juice and olive oil, stir in the parsley and season with salt and pepper. Pour over the vegetables, toss well and serve with slices of lamb.

Conventional cooking: Roast the lamb at 190C/375F/Gas mark 5.

Cook's note
You can butterfly lamb yourself with a good sharp knife. Slit underneath the joint to the bone and cut and scrape all the meat off the bone as you loosen it. Use the bone for stock or gravy.

Rack of Lamb with a Herb Crust

Rack of lamb is a special joint, delicately flavoured. Here I have used a light herby breadcrumb coating – the fresh herb flavour complements the new season's lamb beautifully. This recipe may seem daunting at first glance, but a lot can be prepared several days ahead. You may need to give your butcher notice of how you would like the joint trimmed. Ask him to remove the chine bone and 'French' trim the joints. Keep the trimmings for the jus.

2 racks of lamb from the
    best end or neck end,
    about 8 ribs each
2 tablespoons vegetable oil
2 tablespoons Dijon
    mustard
Provencal breadcrumbs
    (see page 133)

Serves 4

For the jus
Bones and trimmings from
    the lamb
1 tablespoon vegetable oil
$^1/_2$ small onion, peeled and
    chopped
1 clove garlic, peeled and
    crushed
1 large tomato, chopped
1 tablespoon tomato purée
Salt and pepper

Make the jus or gravy. This can be done a day or two before cooking the meat and re-heating as needed.

Put the bones and trimming in a small roasting tin and drizzle over the oil. Hang the roasting tin on the second set of runners from the top of the roasting oven and cook the bones for about 20 minutes, until browned. Stir the chopped onion, garlic, tomato and tomato purée in to the bone mixture and season with salt and pepper. Return to the oven for 15 minutes and then stand the tin on the simmering plate. Scrape all the bits that may have stuck to the base of the tin and add 200ml/7fl oz water to the tin. Allow the stock to bubble for a few minutes and then return to the floor of the roasting oven for about 20–30 minutes. By this time the stock will have reduced. Strain the stock through a fine sieve. Taste the stock. If you like the flavour use the stock as it is or thicken with a teaspoonful of cornflour. Or you may wish to reduce the stock further for a richer flavour. If you like, chill the stock and reserve until needed. Return to the boil before serving.

Prepare the lamb. Put the lamb in a roasting tin and hang the tin on the second set of runners from the top of the roasting oven for 12–15 minutes. Remove from the oven and smear with the mustard. Press over the breadcrumbs. At this stage the lamb can be left in a cool place for 3–4 hours.

When ready to finish the cooking, hang the roasting tin on the second set of runners from the top of the roasting oven for 8–10 minutes (for pink lamb), 12–14 minutes (for well done lamb). Allow to stand somewhere warm for 5 minutes before carving.

Re-heat the jus, carve the racks and serve with roast vegetables.
Conventional cooking: Roast the lamb at 200C/400F/Gas mark 6.

Roast Mutton

Mutton has more flavour than a lot of lamb but for roasting choose a prime joint as it won't be quite as tender as lamb.

Leg of mutton
2 large potatoes, peeled and
   sliced
2 large onions, peeled and
   sliced

2 sprigs rosemary
Salt and pepper
300ml/½ pint cider or
   apple juice

Put the potatoes and onions in the base of a roasting tin. Lay on the rosemary sprigs and season with salt and pepper. Lay the mutton joint on top of the vegetables and pour round the cider or apple juice.

Hang the tin on the bottom set of runners of the roasting oven and roast the mutton for 25 minutes per 450g/1lb plus 25 minutes.

Remove from the tin and allow to rest for 20–30 minutes while making the gravy. Discard the rosemary. Spoon the vegetables into a serving dish and make gravy in the usual way using all the pan juices and either stock or more cider or apple juice to deglaze the pan and reduce to your preferred gravy consistency.

Conventional cooking: Roast in a pre-heated oven at 170C/325F/Gas mark 3.

Cook's note
More vegetables can be cooked in the base of the roasting tin if you like or add a variety of root vegetables. If they are very well cooked they can be served as a mash.

Roasting Beef in the Aga

Beef is considered the King of Roasts and the most British of meats. Beef more than any other meat, must come from a butcher who cares about the meat he sells. If you want to put a good roast beef meal on the table the starting point will be the meat you buy.

A good butcher will know where his meat comes from, he will probably have a good rapport with local farmers and choose cattle on the hoof. The roasting joints come from the animal that moves least – the muscle along the top and back of the beast and the rump end. Then comes careful slaughtering and hanging. Hanging beef is vital for tenderness and flavour. Avoid bright red beef joints, the longer the meat is hung the darker the meat and the more tender the meat on your plate. This hanging of the meat does allow the meat to dry out, so well hung meat tends to be more expensive than freshly slaughtered meat but there again it won't shrink so much when cooking.

So look for a darker joint with a creamy coloured layer of fat. A grass-fed animal will have almost yellow fat. This layer of fat keeps the joint moist but also means that you won't need to baste the joint. The joint should be marbled with thin strands of fat. This also keeps the joint moist and adds flavour. This too is a sign of a well cared for animal. Buying any joint on the bone gives a sweeter roast, so the ultimate roast beef has to be a rib in the bone.

Other joints of beef can, of course, be roasted and it may be worth keeping that rib of beef for special occasions and choosing a cheaper cut for more everyday roasting. So fore-rib and sirloin are the prime roasting joints. Fillet is tender but has a tendency to dryness. Topside and silverside, though often sold for roasting do have a tendency to dryness but will benefit from longer slower roasting and will still taste good.

On the bone or off? A bone helps to conduct heat and will help to cook a joint evenly as well as adding flavour. A boned and rolled joint is easier to carve. Whichever you choose 20–30 minutes resting the joint out of the oven before carving will give justice to the meat. The resting allows the juices to return to the deepest part of the joint which also allows flavours to be absorbed and the meat to be more tender. Don't worry about the joint becoming cold, a reasonable sized joint holds its heat. Keep the roast alongside the Aga during its resting time.

Classic roast beef

If the joint you have chosen doesn't have much fat on it ask the butcher to tie on a piece of fat, it will help baste the meat during cooking and can be removed before serving.

Stand the joint in a roasting tin and rub it with some pepper and mustard. I usually use dry mustard powder for this task.

Calculate the roasting time as follows:

On the bone
Very rare: 12 minutes per 450g/1lb plus 12 minutes
Rare: 15 minutes per 450g/1lb plus 15 minutes
Medium: 20 minutes per 450g/1lb plus 20 minutes
Very well done: 25 minutes per 450g/1lb plus 25 minutes

Off the bone and rolled
Very rare: 15 minutes per 450g/1lb plus 15 minutes
Rare: 20 minutes per 450g/1lb plus 20 minutes
Medium: 25 minutes per 450g/1lb plus 25 minutes
Very well done: 30 minutes per 450g/1lb plus 30 minutes

Hang the roasting tin on the third set of runners from the top of the roasting oven and roast for the calculated time. After half the cooking time check to see that the surface isn't getting too dark. If it is move to the bottom set of runners in the oven or slide a piece of foil or butter paper loosely over the top. Remember that sliding a tray of potatoes to roast above the joint may mean adding an extra 5–10 minutes to the cooking time.

To test if the joint is done to your liking:

Plunge a skewer into the middle of the joint. Leave for 30 seconds. Remove and place against your lip or wrist. If cold, the meat is not done; if warm the meat is rare; if fairly hot the meat is medium done; if hot the meat is well done.

Alternatively, a temperature probe will read: rare at 55–60C; medium at 60–65C; and well done at 65–75C.

Remove the joint from the oven and put on a warm plate to rest while making the gravy and heating through the Yorkshire puddings to serve it with, along with horseradish sauce.

Conventional cooking: Roast in a pre-heated oven at 220C/425F/Gas mark 7.

Meat

Roast Beef in Beer

Beef and ale of 'Olde England' go well together in this recipe. Adding some liquid during cooking helps the rolled and boned joint remain moist as well as giving flavoursome juices for the gravy.

1.25kg/2½lbs joint of boned and rolled rib of beef
2 red onions, peeled and sliced
600ml/1 pint English traditional beer

300ml/½ pint beef or vegetable stock
1–2 tablespoons flour
Salt and pepper
Pinch of sugar

Serves 4–6

Calculate the roasting time: 30 minutes per 450g/1lb plus 30 minutes.

Place the sliced onions in the base of the small roasting tin and put the joint of beef on top. Pour over 300ml/½ pint beer. Hang the tin on the bottom set of runners of the roasting oven and roast for half the calculated cooking time.

At the end of the first half of the cooking time pour round the remaining beer and return to the oven.

At the end of the roasting time remove the meat to a warm plate to rest before carving. Spoon the onions into a dish, draining as much of the juices as possible. Keep warm. Pour the juices from the tin and reserve to make the gravy.

Sprinkle some flour into the base of the tin and scrape in any crusty bits. Slowly whisk in the reserved pan juices and the stock. Stand the tin on the simmering plate and allow the gravy to come to the boil.

Taste the gravy and season with salt and pepper if needed. Add a pinch of sugar if needed. The beer sometimes makes a slightly bitter gravy, this depend largely on the type of beer used. Adjust the seasoning.

Carve the meat and serve with the onions and beery gravy.

Conventional cooking: Pre-heat the oven and roast at 180C/350F/Gas mark 4.

Cook's note
You may prefer to cook a less expensive rolled joint in the same way. Cook it slightly longer for absolute tenderness.

Garlic Beef

Skirt beef is a an under-rated joint that is very versatile. Butchers who butcher their own meat will sell skirt a roasting joint, otherwise it is often cut up and sold as braising steak. Choose a thick piece and take care not to over-cook it.

*1 tablespoons black
peppercorns
6 cloves garlic, peeled*

*2 tablespoons balsamic
vinegar
700g/1¹/₂lb piece trimmed
beef skirt*

Serves 4

Crush the peppercorns and garlic together in a pestle and mortar to make a smooth-ish paste. If you do not have a pestle and mortar grind the peppercorns in your usual grinder and crush the garlic in the usual way and then work together in a basin. Blend in the vinegar.

Stand the meat in a non-metallic dish and rub all over with the peppercorn mixture. Leave to marinade for 1–2 hours.

Heat a baking tray on the floor of the roasting oven for 2–3 minutes and then place the marinated skirt on the hot tray. Return to the floor of the roasting oven for 5 minutes. Turn over the meat and cook the second side for 5–8 minutes, depending upon the thickness of the meat.

Lift the meat onto a carving board and stand for 4–5 minutes and then cut into thin slices. The meat should be pink but not bloody in the middle. Take care not to overcook the meat as it can easily become dry and tough.

Conventional cooking: Pre-heat a ridged pan on the hob until searingly hot and cook the skirt for 4–5 minutes on each side.

Cook's note
Be sure to trim the joint of any excess fat and sinew before preparing for the oven.

Beef Fillet with Glazed Red Onions

Beef fillet is an expensive joint so cook it carefully and treat it with the respect it deserves. Start by asking your butcher for a fillet that is of even thickness throughout its length.

*1.5kg/3lb 5oz joint of beef
   fillet
1kg/2¼lb red onions
75ml/3fl oz balsamic
   vinegar*

*Freshly ground black
   pepper
2 tablespoons olive oil
2–3 sprigs thyme
1 tablespoon chopped
   parsley*

Serves 8

Choose a joint of beef that is more or less an even thickness throughout for even cooking.

Peel the onions but leave the roots intact. Cut the onions in half from the top through to the root and then each half into three.

Grind plenty of black pepper and coat the fillet with it, pressing it in well. Lay the meat in a roasting tin, put the onions around it and tuck the thyme in to the onions. Drizzle the olive oil over the meat and the onions.

Hang the tin on the second set of runners from the top of the roasting oven and cook for 40–45 minutes in total, this will give a medium cooked joint.

After 20 minutes pour half the vinegar over the onions.

When the meat is cooked remove from the oven to a warm board or plate and leave to rest for 15–20 minutes. Pour the remaining vinegar over the onions and stir gently. Put the tin on the floor of the roasting oven, allowing the onions to caramelise.

Slice the beef and serve with the caramelised onions scattered with chopped parsley.

Cook's note
Have the oven up to temperature when cooking this fillet of beef as it needs to be cooked quickly for best results.

Conventional cooking: Pre-heat the oven and roast at 200C/400F/Gas mark 6

Port-glazed Topside of Beef

This is a simple and delicious recipe that adds extra flavour and an attractive look to a run of the mill roasting joint.

1.5kg/3½lbs beef topside or silverside joint
1 clove garlic, peeled and cut into slivers

150ml/¼ pint port
2 tablespoons clear honey
350g/12oz shallots, peeled
Salt and pepper

Serves 4–6

Make a few slits in the beef joint and insert the slivers of garlic. Stand the joint in a small roasting tin.

Mix together the port and honey and pour over the joint. Put the peeled shallots round the joint and season them well.

Hang the roasting tin on the third set of runners from the top of the roasting oven and roast the joint for 25 minutes per 450g/1lb plus 25 minutes.

Periodically spoon some of the juices over the meat to flavour and glaze it.

Remove the meat from the oven and leave to rest on a warm platter close to the Aga for 10–15 minutes before carving.

Serve with the roasted shallots and any juices from the pan.

Conventional cooking: Pre-heat the oven and roast at 190C/375F/Gas mark 5

Cook's note
For ease of peeling put the shallots in a basin and cover with boiling water. Leave to stand for a minute or two then slip off the skins.

Oriental-style Roast Beef

Add some fantastic oriental flavours to roast beef and serve with mashed potatoes that have had chilli sauce stirred into them before serving.

1.3kb/3lb beef topside joint
Salt and pepper
2 teaspoon fennel seeds,
    crushed
2 teaspoon ground
    cinnamon
3 onions, peeled and
    quartered
1–2 tablespoons vegetable
    oil

For the glaze
6 tablespoons hoisin sauce
4 tablespoons orange juice
2.5cm/1 inch cube fresh
    ginger, peeled and grated
2 tablespoons sweet chilli
    sauce

For the gravy
1–2 tablespoons plain flour
600ml/1 pint beef stock
2 tablespoons sherry

Serves 6

Calculate the roasting time
Rare: 20 minutes per 450g/1lb plus 20 minutes
Medium: 25 minutes per 450g /1lb plus 25 minutes
Well done: 30 minutes per 450g/1lb plus 30 minutes

In a bowl mix together the fennel seeds, cinnamon and salt and pepper. Rub this well over the joint of meat. Place the joint in a roasting tin and put the onions around the joint. Drizzle 1–2 tablespoons vegetable oil over them. Hang the tin on the third set of runners from the top of the roasting oven.

30 minutes before the calculated end of roasting time mix the glaze ingredients together in a basin and brush over the joint. Return to the roasting oven for the remaining time.

Remove the meat from the oven and place on a plate with the roast onions and keep warm. Shake or sieve the flour into the roasting tin and stir with a whisk, gradually adding the stock. When the gravy is smooth stand the roasting tin on the simmering plate and allow the gravy to come to the boil, whisking periodically. When the gravy is smooth and thickened stir in the sherry.

Slice the beef and serve with the onions, seasonal green vegetables and the gravy.

Conventional cooking: Pre-heat the oven and roast at 180C/160C Fan/350F/ Gas mark 4

Cook's notes
Topside can be a little dry and tough. If you have a 3 or 4 oven Aga put the joint into the baking oven after 1 hour and increase the cooking time by 45 minutes to 1 hour. This allows for slightly slower, gentler roasting.

Summer Beef with Herbs

This joint of beef is equally delicious whether eaten hot or cold, but the crucial thing is to have a good joint and not to overcook it. If I am serving this with a salad I like to have the meat rare.

1.3kg/3lb joint beef
    silverside or sirloin joint
4–5 tablespoons chopped
    basil or oregano
4 tablespoons chopped
    parsley

6 cloves garlic, peeled and
    crushed
6 tablespoons olive oil
Salt and pepper

Serves 4–6

In a bowl mix together the chopped basil or oregano , parsley, garlic, olive oil and a seasoning of salt and pepper.

Score the skin of the beef and rub the herb mixture in well. Stand in a non-metallic dish, cover and put in the fridge to marinate for 2–3 hours or overnight.

Place the joint in a roasting tin and hang on the third set of runners from the top of the roasting oven for the following times:

Rare: 15 minutes per 450g/1lb plus 15 minutes

Medium: 20 minutes per 450g/1lb plus 20 minutes

Well Done: 25 minutes per 450g/1lb plus 25 minutes

If the joint is browning too much slide a loose piece of foil over the top part way through roasting.

Remove from the oven and if serving hot leave to rest for 10–15 minutes before carving.

If serving cold allow to cool slowly and then chill, covered, until needed.

Conventional cooking: Roast at 200C/400F/Gas mark 6

Cook's note
If the joint is long and thin it will need a slightly shorter cooking time than a short, chunky joint.

Roasting Veal in the Aga

VEAL offers a fine example of how very illogical and squeamish we Brits can sometimes be when it comes to food ethics. For some reason the idea of eating calves can be repulsive and yet the logic is that without calves we have no milk. The cows need to have calves regularly to produce milk. The bull calves from dairy cattle don't produce good beef so with a surplus of them the farmer has little choice. Most calves are shot when very young because we produce more calves than can be eaten for veal. In the UK we have strict animal welfare rules so veal calves here are well looked after, unlike the standards in most continental countries. By eating British welfare-friendly veal we are providing the perfect answer for the animals.

The meat produced in Britain from welfare-friendly breeding is called Rose veal because the meat is pink rather than white. The meat is tender and the flavour light. Some think it is like pork but unlike pork it can be served lightly cooked to medium rare.

Some butchers don't sell veal so either order it or buy from a good source on the internet or from a supermarket, but ensure it is British veal. It will have a pale rose colour, not white and a small amount of fat that should be ivory white and firm.

Veal is usually quickly cooked as in ecsalopes or slowly cooked as in osso bucco. The joints suitable for roasting are topside, leg, loin, best-end and shoulder and for pot roasting silverside and brisket.

I find that after cooking veal in the Aga it remains moist as long as it is not overcooked. Serve slightly pink. You can bard it with fat or wrap in bacon if liked but this is not essential.

Roast Veal

Veal joints, for obvious reasons, are not usually huge but should produce a good meal for 6–8 people. Take care not to overcook the joint as it will dry out quickly. To keep the meat moist it can be wrapped in fatty bacon, barded with fat or given a moist stuffing.

1kg/2¼lb joint veal for roasting
Thin rashers green streaky bacon
2 onions, peeled and sliced

Serves 4–6

Wrap the joint in the bacon. Put the onions in the base of a small roasting tin and stand the prepared veal joint on top.

Hang the roasting tin on the third set of runners from the top of the roasting oven and cook for 15–20 minutes per 500g/1lb.

When cooked remove from the oven to a warm plate and use the pan juices and onions to make a thin gravy.

Allow the joint to rest for at least 15 minutes before carving.

Conventional cooking: Roast in a pre-heated oven at 190C/375F/Gas mark 5. A temperature probe inserted into the middle of the joint should read 70C.

Cook's note
Veal often benefits from a little acidity so you can smear on some mustard or crème fraîche or tomato before cooking and leave off the bacon.

Game

Game is now a popular and widely available choice for a roast. For a season that is, in the main, confined to just six months of the year it offers a varied and rich bounty.

Roasting Game Birds in the Aga

The most popular game bird is pheasant and in recent years this has become plentiful. Pheasant will sometimes be found in the supermarket but a good butcher who hangs the birds properly is the best source unless you have your own guns. Hanging helps to tenderise the meat and bring out the gamey flavour. Use young birds for roasting as an older bird could be dry and tough. Usually the hen is preferred for eating and will have a flavour stronger than a chicken.

Guinea fowl is also popular now and available in supermarkets and farm shops. Any recipe for pheasant works well with guinea fowl.

Quail, most of which will be farmed is usually eaten fresh and not hung. It has a delicate flavour and is tender so it can be cooked by various methods.

Wood pigeon is popular but it is usually just the breast meat that is cooked.

There are many other game birds; should you have some to cook a specialist game book will give you methods for cooking.

Classic roast pheasant

Place a nut of butter inside the pheasant and cover the breast with rashers of streaky bacon. Stand a roasting tin and hang on the third set of runners from the top of the roasting oven.

Roast for 30–35 minutes. Remove the bacon rashers, dust lightly with a little flour and baste the bird. Return to the oven for 5–10 minutes to brown. Remove from the oven and cut the bird in half lengthways with game shears or good kitchen scissors.

Serve a half pheasant per person with thin gravy and game chips.

Conventional cooking: Pre-heat the oven to 200C/400F/Gas mark 6. Guinea fowl can be cooked in exactly this same way.

Normandy Pheasant

Recipes for this classic recipe of pheasant with apples, cream and calvados are many. This recipe looks very appealing when served with the apple slices. Alternatively the apples could be cooked and then sieved into the sauce.

75g/3oz butter
2 pheasant, oven-ready
4 Cox's apples, cored and sliced but with peel still on
6 tablespoons Calvados

150ml/¹/₄ pint pheasant or chicken stock
300ml/¹/₂ pint crème fraîche or double cream
Salt and pepper

Serves 6

Melt 50g/2oz butter in the small roasting tin on the simmering plate. Brown the pheasants all over and then put them side by side in the tin. Hang the roasting tin on the third set of runners from the top of the roasting oven and roast for 45 minutes.

About 10 minutes before the end of the roasting time heat the remaining 25g/1oz butter in a frying pan on the simmering plate and brown the apple slices. Move the apple slices to a platter and keep warm in the simmering oven.

Remove the cooked pheasant to the platter of apples and keep warm while making the sauce. Stand the roasting tin on the simmering plate and pour n the Calvados. Allow it to heat through and then ignite with a match. When the flames die down add the stock and allow to bubble and reduce a little. Whisk in the crème fraîche or cream and bubble to make a glossy sauce. Adjust the seasoning.

Carve the pheasant and serve with apple slices and Calvados sauce.

Conventional cooking: Pre-heat the oven to 200C/400F/Gas mark 6.

Cook's note
Have a baking tray to hand when flaming the Calvados. Should the flames get out of hand don't move the tin just slide over the baking tray and then move the tin off the heat. Don't peek until everything has cooled down.

Roast Pheasant
in Gin with a Fruit Stuffing

Gin goes surprisingly well with the pheasant. See if your guests can guess the flavouring!

2 pheasant
1 tablespoon olive oil
6 rashers streaky bacon
100ml/3^1/$_2$ fl oz gin
100ml/3^1/$_2$ fl oz water

For the stuffing
2 Cox's apples, cored and
   chopped

110g/4oz ready-to-eat dried
   apricots, chopped
8 juniper berries, crushed
2 shallots, peeled and finely
   chopped
1 tablespoon chopped
   parsley
2 tablespoons gin
Salt and pepper

Serves 4–6

Mix all the stuffing ingredients together well. Stuff the pheasant and tie the legs together. Rub the olive oil all over the pheasant and lay the streaky bacon rashers over the breasts. Stand the prepared pheasant in a roasting tin and hang on the third set of runners from the top of the roasting oven for 45 minutes to 1 hour. Mix together the gin and the water and use this to baste the birds throughout their roasting time.

   Remove the bacon from the breasts of the birds for the last 10 minutes to allow even browning.

   Any pan juices can be spooned over the carved meat.

   Serve with game chips or hand-cut crisps and seasonal vegetables.

Conventional cooking: Pre-heat the oven to 190C/375 /Gas mark 5 and roast as above.

Cook's note
Don't truss the birds too tightly, the stuffing needs room to expand and the heat needs to get into the birds to cook them.

Roast Partridge
with Apricot and Sausagemeat Dumplings

Partridges are small and you need one per person. To add flavour and some extra meat for those that like it I have added little dumplings to accompany.

4 partridges
8 rashers streaky bacon
40g/1½ oz dried ready-to-eat apricots, chopped
225g/8oz sausagemeat

2 tablespoons chopped parsley
1 tablespoon flour
250ml/8fl oz vegetable or chicken stock
Salt and pepper

Serves 4

Wrap 2 rashers bacon over each partridge and secure with a cocktail stick. Stand the partridges in a small roasting tin.

In a basin mix together the apricots, sausagemeat, parsley and a seasoning of salt and pepper. When well mixed divide the mixture into eight balls. Put in the roasting tin around the partridges.

Hang the roasting tin on the third set of runners from the top of the roasting oven for 40 minutes. At the end of the roasting time move the partridges and the dumplings onto a warmed serving plate.

Sprinkle the flour into the roasting tin and scrape up any sediment. Gradually whisk in the stock. Stand the tin on the simmering plate and allow the gravy to boil and thicken.

Serve the partridges with the dumplings and the gravy.

Conventional cooking: Roast the partridge in a pre-heated oven at 190C/375F/Gas mark 5 for 40 minutes.

Cook's note
If the sausagemeat has given off a lot of fat during cooking drain some off before making the gravy.

Roast Grouse
with a Blackberry Sauce

The grouse season really gets going about the time of the first blackberries ripening, so it seems sensible to eat them together!

2 dressed grouse
Salt and pepper
25g/1oz butter

For the sauce
225g/8oz blackberries
4 tablespoons grouse or

chicken stock
1 tablespoon lemon juice
1 tablespoon crème de
    Cassis
1 teaspoon corn flour

Serves 2

Wipe the grouse and season inside. Smear the outside with the butter and stand in a small roasting tin. Hang the tin on the third set of runners from the top of the roasting oven and roast for 30–35 minutes.

Meanwhile prepare the sauce. Put the blackberries in a saucepan with the stock and the lemon juice. Stand on the simmering plate and bring slowly to the boil. Simmer for about 5 minutes and crush the blackberries as they cook.

Remove the grouse from the oven and put on a warm plate while completing the sauce. Strain the cooked blackberries in to the roasting tin and stir on the simmering plate, scraping up any crusty pan juices. Blend the crème de Cassis with the corn flour and whisk in to the sauce. Allow to bubble and thicken.

Serve the grouse with some sauce poured round and the remaining sauce in a jug separately.

Conventional cooking: Roast in a pre-heated oven at 190C/375F/Gas mark 5 for 35–40 minutes.

Cook's note
This sauce quantity will be enough if you wish to roast up to 4 grouse at a time.

Quail
with a Mushroom Sauce

Quail are tiny birds that do very well as starter portions. I find this recipe works well as a starter if you are doing a light main course or alternatively, if serving two quail per person, as a main course.

4 quail
4 cloves garlic, peeled
1 clove garlic, peeled and crushed
50g/2oz butter, softened
1 tablespoon chopped parsley
Salt and pepper

For the sauce
50g/2oz button mushrooms, finely sliced
50g/2oz brown cap mushrooms, finely sliced
25g/1oz butter
200ml/7fl oz chicken stock
1 tablespoon chopped parsley

Serves 4 as a starter, 2 as a main course.

Place a whole clove of garlic in each quail. Put the quail in a small roasting tin. Set aside.

Beat together the crushed garlic, softened butter, parsley and a seasoning of salt and pepper. Spoon the butter mixture on to a sheet of cling film and form in to a sausage shape. Seal the ends of the cling film and chill or pop in the freezer if time is short.

Hang the quail on the third set of runners from the top of the roasting oven and roast for 25 minutes.

Meanwhile make the sauce. Melt the butter in a saucepan and add the mushrooms. Stir well and cook for about 5 minutes. When the mushrooms are cooked pour over the stock, bring to the boil and simmer for 8–10 minutes. This will allow the stock to reduce. Stir in the parsley and adjust the seasoning.

Spoon some sauce on to a plate and top with a roasted quail. Slice some herby butter and place on top of the birds.

Conventional cooking: Pre-heat the oven to 190C/ 375C/Gas mark 5 and cook as above.

Cook's note
Any remaining butter can be used to top steaks or chops or stirred in to lightly cooked vegetables.

Roast Wild Duck
with a Mushroom Sauce

Wild duck are usually small birds compared with their domesticated cousins. One bird will usually serve 2 and is best served pink. Most wild duck will be mallard.

1 wild duck, about ½ kilo/1lb 2oz
Sprig thyme
Salt and pepper
15g/½oz soft butter

For the mushroom sauce
400g/14oz wild or interesting selection of mushrooms

1 tablespoon olive oil
25g/1oz butter
1 onion, finely chopped
1 clove garlic, finely chopped
1 tablespoon chopped parsley
Salt and pepper
100ml/3½fl oz white wine

Serves 2

Put the sprig of thyme in the cavity of the duck. Season with salt and pepper and rub the butter over the duck. Place in a roasting tin.

Hang the tin on the second set of runners from the top of the roasting oven and roast for 10 minutes. Then move the tin to the bottom set of runners for 20–30 minutes.

Remove from the oven and allow to rest for 10 minutes before carving.

For the mushroom sauce, pick over the mushrooms and remove any grit or soil. Do not wash. Slice or tear into pieces.

Heat the olive oil and butter in a saucepan and add the onion and garlic. Cook gently until soft but not brown. Stir in the mushrooms and sauté until the mushrooms have collapsed. Add the parsley, a seasoning of salt and pepper and the wine. Bring the sauce to a bubble and allow to reduce until the mushrooms have a little liquid around them.

Cook's note
Take care not to overcook the meat otherwise it will be as tough as old boots!

Conventional cooking: Start in a pre-heated oven at 230C/450F/Gas mark 8 for 10 minutes and then turn the oven down to 180C/350F/Gas mark 4 for the remaining cooking time.

Roasting Rabbit and Hare in the Aga

The rabbits that are best for eating are wild animals caught and sold by reputable butchers and dealers, not the imported varieties which usually come frozen and jointed and can be found in supermarkets.

For roasting hare use a whole animal (usually dressed by your butcher). You will need a young animal, so if it is still complete look for sharp teeth and claws and soft ears. Hare is often hung for 2 to 3 days before skinning and the blood collected for thickening the sauce.

Roast Rabbit

For roasting make sure your butcher supplies you with a young rabbit otherwise it will be tough.

1 whole rabbit, skinned and head removed	*lightly crushed*
Salt and pepper	*50g/2oz softened butter*
2 sprigs thyme	*2 tablespoons Dijon*
2 cloves garlic, peeled and	*mustard*

A whole rabbit will serve 3–4 people

Put the thyme and the garlic cloves in the body cavity of the rabbit or hare and season inside and out with salt and pepper. Smear the softened butter all over the outside. Lay in a roasting tin.

Hang the roasting tin on the bottom set of runners of the roasting oven and roast for 15 minutes. Baste the rabbit with the pan juices. Cook for a further 30 minutes and then smear with the mustard and baste well. Return to the oven for a further 15 minutes. Remove from the oven and leave to rest on a warm plate while making the gravy. If you like you can de-glaze the roasting tin with a little brandy before making a small amount of sauce.

Conventional cooking: Pre-heat the oven to 200C/400F/Gas mark 6.

Cook's note
Use the chicken stock to make a gravy to serve with this roast.

Roast Hare

Hare for roasting needs to be a young hare and usually just the saddle and possibly the hind quarters will be roasted. The rest can be made into stock and the heart and liver can go into a stuffing if you like. A saddle of hare will usually serve 2 people.

1 saddle of hare
2 tablespoons sunflower oil
Salt and pepper
4 juniper berries, crushed
4 black peppercorns,
  crushed

1 carrot, sliced
1 onion, peeled and sliced
2 sticks celery, sliced
250ml/7fl oz red wine

Serves 2

Put 1 tablespoon of sunflower oil in the roasting tin and stand on the simmering plate. Stir in the juniper berries, peppercorns, carrot, onion and celery. Stir round until the vegetables are starting to soften.

Rub the remaining tablespoon of oil over the saddle of hare and lay on top of the vegetables. Season with salt and pepper. Pour the wine round the hare and over the vegetables.

Hang the roasting tin on the second set of runners from the top of the roasting oven and roast for 20–25 minutes. Move the roasting tin to the simmering oven for a further 10 minutes.

Allow to rest for 5–10 minutes before carving and serving on the bed of vegetables. The meat should be slightly pink.

Conventional cooking: Roast at 220C/425F/Gas mark 7 and turn off the oven for the last 10 minutes.

Cook's note
A young hare is best for roasting so it should be possible to get two saddles together in one roasting tin.

Roasting Venison in the Aga

Venison is the meat from deer and much under-rated. Over the last twenty or so years, deer farming has become more popular and the demand for venison has increased. This may be because it has a low fat content, about 5% compared with beef at 20% or lamb at 25%. The other side of this is that it has a tendency to dryness as it is so lean so some extra fat or slow and gentle cooking is essential. A joint to be roasted needs marinating or larding with fat or basting during cooking. This may sound complicated but is not. Some butchers will lard the joint for you otherwise marinade the joint overnight and tie some pork back fat round the joint before roasting. Venison is probably the only roast that I bother to baste during roasting and is well worth the effort.

The best place to buy venison is the Farmer's Market or farm shops where it is usually sold by the producer who knows about correct hanging. Farmed venison tends to be more tender than wild venison. Fore-quarter and saddle of venison will be a sweet meat and haunch (rear leg of the deer) will often be tender.

Roast Haunch of Venison

A special occasion roast that brings out the very best in venison. The long marinating process is essential so don't be tempted to scrimp on time!

1 haunch venison
Pork back fat for larding,
    cut into fine strips or in
    the piece to tie over the
    joint

For the marinade
1 litre /1³/₄ pints red wine
1 onion, peeled and finely
    chopped

4 tablespoons olive oil
2 bay leaves
1 sprig rosemary
1 sprig thyme
6 juniper berries, lightly
    crushed
10 peppercorns, lightly
    crushed

Mix the marinade ingredients together in a large non-metallic bowl and add the haunch of venison. Leave to marinate overnight, turning the joint if necessary.

Remove the joint from the marinade and lard with strips of fat and a larding needle or simply tie on the pieces of fat. Place the joint in a roasting tin and pour over the marinade. Season with a little salt and pepper.

Hang the roasting tin on the third set of runners from the top of the roasting oven for 20 minutes. Baste. Then put the shelf on the floor of the oven and put the tin on that, or if you have a 3- or 4-oven Aga hang the tin on the second set of runners from the bottom of the baking oven.

Roast the joint for a further 10 minutes per 450g/1lb.

Remove the joint from the oven and leave to rest on a warm plate for 15 minutes before carving. Remove any extra covering of barding fat before carving. The meat should be pink in the middle otherwise it will be too dry.

Make the gravy from the marinade juices in the roasting tin .

Conventional cooking: Pre-heat the oven to 220C/425F/Gas mark 7 for the first 20 minutes and then reduce the temperature to 160C/325F/Gas mark 3 for the remaining time.

Cook's note
Ask your butcher to lard the joint if you don't feel able to do it yourself.

Orange and Rosemary-glazed Venison

This is a perfect recipe for a joint of farmed venison. It won't need larding and can be cooked like rare beef, but do take care not to overcook otherwise it will become dry.

1 boneless venison joint
3 tablespoons orange marmalade
1¹/₂ tablespoons chopped

rosemary leaves
150ml/¹/₄ pint beef or vegetable stock
Salt and pepper

Serves 6

Calculate the cooking time. Cook as high as possible in the roasting oven for 15 minutes and then move to the bottom set of runners of the roasting oven for 10 minutes per 450g/1lb for very rare or 15 minutes per 450g/1lb if you prefer medium to well-done.

Meanwhile put the marmalade and rosemary in a saucepan and allow to soften. Mix well together with a seasoning of salt and pepper. Remove from the heat.

15 minutes before the end of cooking spoon half the glaze over the joint of venison and return to the oven for the rest of the roasting time.

Remove the joint to a warm plate and allow to rest for at least 20 minutes before carving.

Pour the remaining glaze into the roasting tin with the stock and stand on the simmering plate. Allow to come to the boil, simmer for 2–3 minutes and pour over the joint before serving.

Conventional cooking: Pre-heat the oven to 220C/425F/Gas mark 7 and cook the venison for the first 15 minutes. Then reduce the oven temperature to 180C/350F/Gas mark 4 for the remaining roasting time.

Cook's note
You will need to increase the glaze quantities if you would like to serve the glaze as a sauce with the meat.

Fish

Fish roasts beautifully in the Aga, be it whole fish or fillets. Roasting enhances all of the myriad wonderful flavours that fish has to offer and it really couldn't be any easier than the recipes which follow.

Roasting Fish in the Aga

Roasting brings out the flavour of fish and is an easy method of cooking fish.

It is easier to cook a large fish in the oven than on the hob and of course all the smells from cooking fish will whizz out of the chimney and not into the kitchen.

Use a baking tray to lay the fish on and cook towards the top of the oven if you wish to crisp the skin on the top or on the floor for a crisped underneath.

The biggest problem with cooking fish is the danger of overcooking it. Overcooking renders the fish dry in texture and tasteless so it is best to remove the fish from the oven when barely cooked. A few minutes resting will complete the cooking and the flesh will be moist. Cooked fish will just start to flake when a knife is inserted in the thickest part.

Add flavour to your fish with lemon slices or herbs such as tarragon and parsley. Very little oil or fat is needed when roasting fish. Use a lightly flavoured olive oil, sunflower or rapeseed oil. Rub this in to the skin to help crisp the skin. The skin will retain the moistness and enhance the flavour of the flesh and can be removed before serving. Similarly fish cooked on the bone always has an improved flavour. When serving lift off the skin and then lift out the backbone and most of the bones will come out with it. It is then easy to portion out the fish.

Try experimenting with different fish not only salmon but salmon trout, turbot, sea bass and other whole fish that your fishmonger can supply. Ring the changes with a variety of roast vegetables in season to go with the fish.

Poaching salmon and trout

Whole fish is not often roasted on its own. However, you will find a few recipes following on that are for small fillets or small whole fish that are roasted along with other ingredients. Salmon and trout are sometimes roasted whole but usually poached to serve cold so I have decided to put instructions for poaching these fish in the Aga as this is something I am regularly asked about. *However, if the salmon or sea trout is to be served hot it is better to roast the fish for a more pleasing texture.* Most salmon and trout are now farmed and have come down in price. You may be lucky enough to catch your own wild salmon but otherwise wild salmon tends to be more expensive and scarce. It does however have a better flavour and texture than farmed salmon. Try sea trout for good flavour and texture if you can find it, it is superior to farmed salmon.

3kg/6½lb fish will serve 8–10 people.

Use the large roasting tin and a sheet of Bake-O-Glide or foil to help lifting the fish after cooking.

Put the gutted and cleaned fish on a sheet of foil large enough to wrap loosely round the fish. Rub the fish with a little salt and pepper and season the inside. Slice a lemon and put slices inside the fish. Loosely wrap the fish in the foil and lift into the roasting tin. Hang the tin on the bottom set of runners of the roasting oven and pour round a kettle full of boiling water. Leave the fish in the oven for 15 minutes and then remove the tin from the oven. Leave in the tin until completely cold.

Conventional cooking: Place the fish in a fish kettle, usually available to hire from your fishmonger. Add the seasoning and lemon slices. Fill with water and stand on the hob. Bring slowly to the boil and bubble for 2 minutes. Turn off the heat, cover the pan and leave until completely cold. Leave the fish in the kettle until it has completely cooled.

Lift the cold fish out of the tin, unwrap and remove the skin. Place on a large platter to serve with homemade hollandaise sauce or mayonnaise.

Classic roast salmon or trout

Use the large roasting tin and a sheet of Bake-O-Glide or foil to help lift the hot fish from the tin.

Lay out a large sheet of foil and oil with olive oil. Lay on the clean gutted fish. Season with salt and pepper and put slices of lemon inside. Fronds of tarragon or fennel are also good for flavouring. Loosely wrap the fish in the foil and lift into the roasting tin.

Slide the tin onto the bottom set of runners of the roasting oven and cook the fish for 10 minutes per 450g/1lb.

Conventional cooking: Put the fish prepared as above in a pre-heated oven at 190C/170C Fan/375F/Gas Mark5 for 10 minutes per 450g/1lb.

Remove the fish from the oven and unwrap. Remove the skin and serve on a warmed plate. Serve with Hollandaise sauce.

Japanese-style Roast Salmon

Marinating salmon will give salmon an extra dimension. As it is such a commonly eaten fish this recipe rings the changes.

8 tablespoons dark soy sauce
8 tablespoons mirin
4 tablespoons rice wine or dry sherry
5cm/2 inch cube fresh ginger peeled and cut into slivers
Small side of salmon

Serves 4–6

Put the soy sauce, mirin and rice wine together in a basin. Lay the salmon in a non-metallic dish and scatter over half the ginger. Pour over the mixed marinade ingredients. Leave to marinate for half and hour.

Line a baking tray with Bake-O-Glide. Drain the fish from the marinade, reserving the marinade for later. Lay the salmon on the tray, skin side uppermost.

Hang the baking tray on the second set of runners from the top of the roasting oven and roast the fish for 20 minutes. Pull out the tray and brush the fish with the reserved marinade and return to the oven for a further 10 minutes.

The salmon skin should be crispy and a knife inserted in the middle will show that the salmon is cooked. If needed cook for a little longer. Remember that a short plump fillet will take longer to cook than a longer, thinner piece.

When cooked carefully lift the salmon to a warmed serving plate and scatter over the remaining ginger.

Conventional cooking: Roast at 190C/375F/Gas mark 5

Cook's notes
Scrape the skin of the fish with a knife blade from the tail end to remove excess scales before putting to marinate.

Roast Monkfish
with Potatoes and Shallots

Monkfish is a firm-fleshed fish that is good for roasting. Usually we buy it in small portions but cooking a whole piece makes a change to the usual roast meats. This recipe has the flavours of the south of France and is perfect for hot summer days.

1 large piece of tail-end monkfish, about 1kg/2lb 4oz	*4 cloves garlic, peeled and slivered*
16 small potatoes, washed	*4–5 sprigs thyme, leaves stripped from the stalk*
12 shallots, peeled	*150ml/5fl oz white wine*
Salt and pepper	*Grated rind 1 orange*
Juice 2 lemons	*2 tablespoons chopped parsley*
100ml/3¹/₂ fl oz olive oil	

Serves 4–6

Put the potatoes and shallots in a saucepan with a pinch of salt and the juice of 1 lemon. Add enough water to come 2.5cm/1 inch up the side of the saucepan. Cover the pan and stand on the boiling plate. Bring the vegetables to the boil and drain off all the water. Re-cover and put in the simmering oven for 20–30 minutes, until the potatoes are only just cooked. Drain well and then return to the saucepan. Add 3–4 tablespoons of olive oil and toss the vegetables. Tip into the base of a roasting tin.

Make some slits in the flesh of the monkfish and push in some garlic slivers (don't push them all the way in as they will be removed later). Put the monkfish in the tin with the potatoes and shallots. Drizzle over 2–3 tablespoons of olive oil, about half the thyme leaves and a seasoning of salt and pepper.

Hang the roasting tin on the bottom set of runners of the roasting oven and roast the fish for 35–40 minutes until cooked. Insert a sharp pointed knife into the thickest part of the fish, if it comes out warm then the fish is cooked. Remove the fish to a warmed plate and return the roasting tin to the oven, on the second set of runners from the top for 5–10 minutes until the vegetables are golden brown.

Meanwhile pull the garlic slivers out of the fish and put in a small saucepan with the white wine, juice of the second lemon and the orange zest. Stand on the simmering plate and allow to bubble until reduced by half. Stir in the remaining olive oil, thyme and parsley. Spoon over the monkfish.

Slice the fillets off the bone and cut each in half. Serve with the roast vegetables.

Conventional cooking: Cook the potatoes and shallots on the hob in the usual way. Pre-heat the oven to 190C/170C Fan/375F/Gas mark 5.

Cook's note
The amount of time it takes to cook the baby potatoes will depend upon their variety. The waxy salad potatoes like Anya and Charlotte will take longer than say a Jersey Royal.

Monkfish
with Spinach and Goats Cheese

Monkfish tails are expensive so this dish is best used for a special meal. This recipe is perfect for entertaining as it really needs time once prepared to set in the fridge before roasting.

150g/5oz fresh spinach
110/4oz soft goats cheese
1 tablespoon pine nuts
2 x 450g/1lb monkfish tails
Salt and pepper

8 slices Parma ham
2 teaspoons Thai curry paste
2 tablespoons mango chutney

Serves 4

Wash the spinach and place in a small saucepan with just the water that is clinging to it. Put on the lid and cook for a few minutes until wilted. Remove from the heat, drain well and chop. Put the spinach in a basin with the goats cheese and pine nuts. Mix together and season with salt and pepper.

Place one monkfish tail on the work surface and spread the spinach filling down the middle. Lay on the second monkfish tail to form a sandwich. Lay out the strips of ham, stand on the monkfish and wrap it well in the ham.

Stand the monkfish on a baking tray lined with Bake-O-Glide. Cover and chill for 1 hour.

To cook, hang the baking tray on the third set of runners from the top of the roasting oven and bake the monkfish for 20–25 minutes, until crisp on the outside and the fish cooked through.

Place the curry paste and the chutney in a small saucepan, stir well and heat through. Stir in any pan juices.

Slice the monkfish and serve with a spoonful of chutney sauce.

Conventional cooking: Pre-heat the oven to 180C/350F/Gas mark 4 and roast for 20–25 minutes until the fish is crisp on the outside and the fish is cooked through.

Cook's note
Serve with new potatoes and a simple vegetable to enhance the flavours of the fish.

Roast Cod
with Winter Vegetables

Most of us tend to use summer vegetables with fish but root vegetables and squashes work just as well in the autumn and winter. Try to buy cod fillets with skin on – it will crisp and taste more succulent.

4 thick cod fillets, skin on
2 parsnips, peeled and cut
*   into small-ish pieces*
1 small butternut squash,
*   peeled and the flesh*
*   cubed*

2 potatoes, washed and cut
*   into wedges*
4 or 5 stalks fresh sage
5 tablespoons olive oil
50g/2oz pumpkin or
*   sunflower seeds*
Salt and pepper

Serves 4

Put the vegetables in a small roasting tin. Pull the leaves off 2 stalks of sage and add to the vegetables. Drizzle over 2 tablespoons olive oil and stir to coat the vegetables. Hang the roasting tin on the second set of runners from the top of the roasting oven and roast for 15 minutes. Then check the vegetables, stirring if needed and if browning too much move the tin to a lower setting. Roast for a further 10 minutes.

Chop the remaining sage leaves.

Remove the vegetables from the oven and add the chopped sage and the pumpkin seeds. Stir gently.

Brush the cod fillets with the remaining olive oil and lay skin side uppermost on the vegetables. Return the tin to the second set of runners from the top of the roasting oven.

Roast for 15 minutes by which time the fish will be cooked and the skin crispy.

Serve immediately.

Conventional cooking: Pre-heat the oven and roast at 200C/180Fan/400F/Gas mark 6.

Cook's note
Add variety by using different vegetables such as carrots, onions and sweet potatoes.

Italian Roast Fish
with Olives and Tomatoes

*This is a simple everyday meal in a dish to remind you of hot summer days!
It is oh-so-easy to prepare.*

25g/1oz butter
1 tablespoon olive oil
1 onion, peeled and sliced
2 cloves garlic, peeled and
   sliced
700g/1$^1/_2$lb King Edward
   potatoes (floury) peeled
   and cut into 2cm /
   $^3/_4$inch dice

6 plum tomatoes, roughly
   chopped
200ml/7 fl oz dry white
   wine
200ml/7 fl oz fish stock
100g/3$^1/_2$oz Italian olives
1kg/2$^1/_4$lb cod fillets in
   6 even portions, brushed
   with a little olive oil
Chopped parsley to garnish

Serves 6

Heat the butter and the oil in a shallow ovenproof dish or roasting tin. Add the
onion and cook for 2–3 minutes before adding the garlic and potato cubes.
Toss in the hot fat and after 1 minute stir in the tomatoes and the wine.
Bubble fast to reduce the wine and then stir in the fish stock and the olives.

   Put the shelf on the second set of runners from the bottom of the roasting
oven and put in the dish of potatoes and tomatoes. Cook for 20–25 minutes, until
the potatoes are tender.

   Nestle the fish onto the potato mixture. Return the pan to the oven and roast
for 7–10 minutes, until the fish is cooked and golden.

   Scatter over the parsley and serve with green beans and warm bread.

Conventional cooking: Start the dish on the hob and then move to a pre-heated
oven when fish stock and olives have been added. Pre-heat the oven to 190C/
375F/Gas mark 5.

Cook's note
Make sure the
potatoes are
cooked before
adding the fish to
the dish. Different
varieties of potato
will take different
amounts of
cooking time.

Roast Sea Bass
with a Walnut Pesto

Sea bass whether wild or farmed has become a very popular fish. Like salmon it sometimes needs a special treatment now that it is so readily available. This dish is easy to prepare and is good all year round, just serve with different accompaniments according to season.

*1–1.5kg/2–3lb whole sea
   bass, cleaned
50g/2oz walnuts, toasted
4 spring onions, trimmed
   and chopped*

*1 clove garlic, peeled
Small bunch parsley
4 tablespoons olive oil
Salt and pepper
Lemon segments to garnish*

Serves 4–6

Make the pesto. Put the walnuts, spring onions, parsley, olive oil and a seasoning of salt and pepper in a blender or food processor and whizz until smooth.

Rinse and dry the sea bass. Cut three diagonal slashes on each side of the fish and lay in a small roasting tin. Spoon some of the pesto into the fish and then smear the rest over the fish.

Hang the roasting tin on the second set of runners from the top of the roasting oven and roast for 25–30 minutes, until the skin is crisp and the flesh is white. Serve the fish on a bed of watercress with lemon segments to garnish.

Conventional cooking: Roast the fish in a pre-heated to 220C/425F/Gas mark 7 and cook for 25–30 minutes.

Cook's note
While making the pesto for this dish you may wish to double the quantity and use the spare pesto as a pasta sauce or for dressing potatoes. Store in the fridge in a jar with a little olive oil on the top to form a seal. It will keep for a month.

Sea Bream with Lemon

Serve this whole roasted fish in the Mediterranean way just with bread to mop up the juices and salad as a separate course. If bream is not available other whole fish such as sea bass can be cooked in the same way.

1 whole sea bream, about
   1.5kg/3lbs 5oz
4 onions, peeled
3 lemons
$^1/_2$ glass white wine

3 tablespoons olive oil
Salt and pepper

Serves 4–6

Slice the onions in half and then into slices. Slice the lemons into thick slices. Wash and dry the fish. Slice 4 or 5 diagonal slashes through the skin on either side of the fish. Slip a lemon slice into each slash and the remaining lemon slices into the cavity. Season with salt and pepper.

   Line a large baking tray with a sheet of Bake-O-Glide and cover it with the onion slices. Lay on the fish and drizzle over the olive oil and the wine.

   Hang the tray of fish on the third set of runners from the top of the roasting oven and cook for 30–40 minutes. To test that the fish is cooked insert the point of a knife into the thickest part of the fish, the flesh will flake slightly and the point of the knife will be hot.

Conventional cooking: Pre-heat the oven to 180C/160C Fan/350F/Gas Mark 4.

Cook's note
The fish can be prepared ahead of time and cooked as needed, but add an extra 5 minutes cooking time if the fish has been kept in the fridge.

Vegetables

Whether as accompaniments to the main attraction or as a meal in their own right, roasting vegetables brings out flavour and provides endless possibilities for enhancing your roast repertoire.

Roasting Vegetables in the Aga

Vegetables add flavours and colour to a roast meal. In this book, with one exception, I have only provided recipes for roast vegetables, which of course don't have to be accompaniments but can be dishes in their own right.

Vegetables that have been roasted in the Aga have a delicious flavour and are so easy to prepare.

The flavours vary according to the seasons but also try using different fats and oils to bring out different flavours. Goose fat, lard and dripping are commonly used for roast potatoes and parsnips but olive oil and that home grown oil, rapeseed oil add different flavours. Ring the changes. Use as little fat as possible to allow the vegetable flavours to sing through. Just enough fat to lightly coat the vegetables, not having them swimming.

The variety of vegetables to accompany a roast is endless. Add variety to your roast meals by choosing vegetables in season. Serve some as a roast and some plainly cooked. I cook green vegetables at the last minute on the boiling plate so that they are bright green and of a very fresh flavour.

Apples

Apple always goes well with roast pork. Instead of making apple sauce I sometimes like to serve whole apples that are roasted around the joint. They are quick and easy to prepare and look attractive.

1 eating apple per person

Core each apple and lightly slit the skin from the top to the middle. 30 minutes before the end of the roasting time for the meat stand the apples around the joint and baste with some of the pan juices. The apples should be tender but still holding their shape when ready to serve.

Beetroot

Beetroot has rightly become fashionable again and is served so differently from the over-boiled variety I had at school every week with boiled fish and potatoes. Roasting beetroot brings out the flavour and it adds a wonderful colour to the plate.

Beetroot
Olive oil

Peel the beetroot. Cut the beetroot into even-sized pieces. Toss in enough olive oil to coat the beetroot. Put the beetroot onto a baking tray lined with Bake-O-Glide and hang on the third set of runners from the top of the roasting oven. Roast for 30–40 minutes until the beetroot is cooked.

Cabbage

Roasting cabbage seems unlikely but Aga owners do like to use the ovens as much as possible so here is a popular recipe from my Traditional Aga Christmas book.

75g/3oz butter
1 shallot, peeled and finely chopped
3 bay leaves
1 large cabbage, trimmed and
* cut into quarters*
100ml/3½fl oz chicken or vegetable
* stock*

Serves 4

Melt the butter in a small saucepan and add the shallot and the bay leaves. Cook gently until the shallot is soft and the butter flavoured. Put the cabbage in a deep baking dish so that it fits snugly. Pour over the shallot pan juices and toss to mix in with the cabbage leaves.

Hang the oven shelf on the bottom set of runners of the roasting oven and put in the cabbage. Roast for 10 minutes and then spoon over the stock and cook for a further 10–15 minutes. Serve the juices over the cabbage when serving.

Carrots

Of all the vegetables that I buy carrots can have the most disappointing flavour. For the best chance of your carrots having a good flavour either grow your own, buy very fresh from a local producer or buy organic. Then bring out any flavour by roasting the carrots which enhances their natural sweetness.

Small, new carrots can be roasted but I think this is a waste so I tend to roast larger main crop carrots.

Carrots can be roasted whole or cut to any size. The cooking time will depend upon the age of the carrot and the size you cut them.

Carrots
25g/1oz butter
1 tablespoon light vegetable oil such as sunflower

Peel the carrots as thinly as possible. Trim the ends. Cut into quarters or leave whole as preferred. Place in a saucepan and add a pinch of salt and enough water to come 2.5cm/ 1 inch up the side of the saucepan. Cover and bring to the boil. Boil for 2–3 minutes and then drain well. Return the carrots to the hot dry pan and add the butter and the oil. Toss well to coat the carrots in the butter and oil.

Tip the carrots on to a baking tray lined with Bake-O-Glide. Hang the tin on the second set of runners from the top of the roasting oven for 20 minutes. Keep an eye on the carrots as they can burn, especially if cut into small sticks.

Serve immediately.

Fennel

Fennel has become more readily available over the last few years. I frequently hear loyal vegetable box customers so often say to me during my Aga demonstrations 'what can I do with fennel, it is so boring just boiled?'
The answer is, of course, to roast with some butter.

Roast fennel goes really well with fish and pork. Any trimmings or blanching water can be used in soups.

Allow 1 bulb of fennel for 2 people
1 tablespoon melted butter for each bulb of fennel

Trim the fennel removing any very hard outer layers. Keep any green fronds to chop later for sprinkling over when serving. Cut each bulb in half from top to bottom and then each half into 2 or 3 slices depending upon the size of the bulb. Try to cut each section with some of the stem intact so all the layers are held together.

Put the fennel into a saucepan and add enough water to come 2.5cm/1 inch up the side of the pan. Season lightly and bring the fennel to the boil. Simmer on the simmering plate until nearly tender. Drain very well and return to the saucepan. Pour over the melted butter and very gently toss to coat the fennel in the butter.

Lay the buttered fennel on a baking tray lined with Bake-O-Glide. Hang the baking tray on the second set of runners from the top of the roasting oven and roast the fennel for about 20 minutes. The fennel should be soft and tingeing with colour.

Spoon into a serving dish and sprinkle on the chopped green fronds.

The roast fennel tastes delicious if some finely grated Parmesan cheese is scattered over it for the last 5 minutes of roasting.

Garlic

Whole heads of roasted garlic can be served with a little salad and some toasted French stick to spread the soft garlic on or stored in olive oil for flavouring soups and sauces. Don't throw away the garlic infused oil, it in lovely for salad dressings.

The roasting takes away the raw flavour and as with most roast vegetables brings out the sweetness, and no you won't smell of garlic for evermore!

1 head of garlic person
1 tablespoons olive oil for each bulb of garlic
Salt and pepper

Trim the top off each bulb of garlic to expose the flesh on the central cloves. Stand the bulbs in an ovenproof dish and brush each bulb generously with the olive oil. Season with salt and pepper.

Put the shelf on the bottom set of runners in the roasting oven and roast the garlic for 30–40 minutes or until the outer skin is crispy and the cloves are soft.

Serve with a small knife or spoon to scoop out the soft cloves.

If you want to preserve the garlic, roast as above and when completely cold put in a jar and cover with olive oil. Alternatively roast the cloves individually, taking about 20 minutes and then store in olive oil.

Mushrooms

In the Bath Farmer's market we have a weekly stall selling 'Dorset Down' mushrooms. Their display of a whole range of mushrooms is tempting and the smell of mushrooms cooking in butter is hard to resist. Sadly the men in my family don't like mushrooms. However, I find if I roast them they add richness to a pasta sauce and they somehow get eaten and enjoyed!

350g/12oz mushrooms, a selection of your choice.
4–5 tablespoons olive oil
Salt and pepper
Sprigs of fresh thyme

Serves 4 as a starter or 6 as an accompaniment

Wipe the mushrooms if they need it but do not wash. Either toss the mushrooms in the olive oil or brush them with the oil. Lay in an ovenproof dish or on a baking tray lined with Bake-O-Glide. Sprinkle over some salt and a grinding of pepper. Tuck the sprigs of thyme amongst the mushrooms.

Hang the baking tray onto the third set of runners from the top of the roasting oven and roast the mushrooms for 25–30 minutes. Serve immediately.

Onions

Roasting onions will bring out their flavour wonderfully. Usually onions are sliced and cooked alongside meat to enhance the flavour and colour of the gravy.

These onions are cooked whole, the outside becomes quite dry and crusty so just the insides are eaten. Red onions in particular look attractive and taste delicious.

10–12 red onions
2–3 tablespoons olive oil

Trim some of the root from each onion so that it will stand level in the tin. Trim the top of the onion and then cut downwards through to the base but not cutting through the root. Cut a second time, thus cutting the onion into quarters. Stand the onions in a roasting tin, fitting as snugly as possible so the onions stay upright. Brush the onions generously with the olive oil.

Hang the roasting tin on the third set of runners from the top of the roasting oven and roast for about 1 hour. When cooked the onions will be slightly blackened on the outside and soft in the middle.

Parsnips

The first parsnips on the market stall at the Farmer's market always signal the start of winter to me and the advent of warming food. They are a versatile vegetable but to my mind the best way to cook and eat them is to roast them.

Parsnips
Goose fat or beef dripping

Peel the parsnips and quarter them lengthways. Only at the very end of winter would I bother to remove the core and only then if it is very tough. Put the parsnips in a saucepan with a pinch of salt. Add enough water to come 2.5cm/ 1 inch up the side of the pan. Stand the pan on the boiling plate and bring to the boil. Simmer for 2–3 minutes and then drain well. Return to the dry pan and add enough fat to lightly coat the parsnips. Toss them to coat in the fat and tip onto a baking tray lined with Bake-O-Glide.

Hang the tray on the second set of runners from the top of the roasting oven and roast for 40 minutes, until cooked and golden brown.

Parmesan parsnips

When the parsnips have been tossed lightly in the fat they can be dusted with finely grated Parmesan cheese which will give them flavour and crunch. Just keep an eye on them so that they don't burn.

Potatoes

Potatoes are usually the main accompanying vegetable for roast meat in some form or other. You can change the seasons by cooking the potatoes in various ways or using different fats, for example goose fat for winter roast potatoes and olive oil for summer roast potatoes.

Roast Potatoes

The first thing to do for successful roast potatoes is to choose the correct potato. A waxy one is not a good idea so go for a floury one like King Edward, Desiree or Maris Piper. These will give a crunchy outer with a fluffy middle.

Peel and cut the potatoes into even-sized portions, allowing on average three pieces per person (unless you are feeding a rugby team!) Put into a large saucepan with a pinch of salt and enough water to come 4cm/ 1½ inches up the side of the pan. There is no need to cover the potatoes in water, it is a waste of water and heat. Cover with a lid and stand the pan on the boiling plate and bring to the boil. Boil the potatoes for 4–5 minutes, until just getting soft on the outside. Drain very well through a colander. When drained really well, return to the dry saucepan and replace the lid. Shake the pan vigorously to fluff up the outside of the potatoes.

Add the chosen fat. For flavour and probably the best roast potatoes I like goose fat, now readily available in supermarkets. However, I also like beef dripping especially with roast beef. Lard also makes a good texture but adds little flavour. Oils can be used but although many people say olive oil isn't good for roast potatoes I do sometimes like it in the height of summer. We have all been taught that the fat must be searingly hot for roast potatoes but I have excellent results and less trouble and mess by adding the cold fat onto the hot potatoes in the saucepan.

So choose the fat and add it to the hot potatoes in the saucepan. Replace the lid and shake the pan to cover all the potatoes in fat. Tip the potatoes onto a flat baking tray lined with Bake-O-Glide. The flat tray allows more heat to the potatoes and they crisp better than those in a roasting tin.

At this stage the potatoes can be set aside somewhere cool until you are ready to cook them. I try to prepare them to this stage the day before cooking so that heat isn't lost from the Aga during preparation.

When ready to roast the potatoes, hang the tray on the second set of runners from the top of the roasting oven. Look at them after 20 minutes, some Agas have a hot spot and the tray may need turning for even browning. Cook for a further 15–20 minutes and then move the tray to the floor of the roasting oven to crisp the potatoes on the base. This saves turning the potatoes. Depending upon the other items in the oven you may want to start on the floor and finish with the potatoes at the top. Serve the potatoes immediately for crispness. Do not put the potatoes in the simmering oven to keep warm, they will loose their crispness and flavour. If the potatoes are ready and you are not then remove from the oven and leave on the worktop. Return to the roasting oven to heat through.

Roast New Potatoes

These potatoes are a quick and easy accompaniment to a summer roast meal.

Wash the potatoes well. If they are large cut to an even size. Dry the potatoes and put in a bowl. Pour on sufficient olive oil to coat the potatoes and then tip onto a baking tray lined with Bake-O-Glide. Sprinkle over a little sea salt and add a sprig of rosemary if liked.

Hang the baking tray on the second set of runners from the top of the roasting oven and roast the potatoes for 40–60 minutes until crisp and cooked through. Serve immediately.

Dauphinois

Although dauphinois potatoes are not roasted they do go very well with some roast meats and make a change from a standard roast potato. I think they are a really good accompaniment to roast lamb.

1kg/2¼lbs potatoes, Desiree or King Edwards work best
Salt and pepper
4 cloves garlic, peeled and finely sliced
600ml/1 pint milk
200ml/7fl oz double cream
1 teaspoon flour

Serves 6

Butter a shallow oven-proof dish, about 850ml/1 ½ pint in volume. Peel the potatoes and slice as thinly as you can. Dry well. Place the potatoes in layers in the dish, seasoning with salt and pepper as you go. Bury the garlic slivers between the layers of potato.

Warm the milk to just below boiling point. Whisk the flour into the cream and then pour the cream into the hot milk. Stir well and then gently pour the milk mixture over the potatoes.

For a two-oven Aga put the shelf on the floor of the roasting oven and put in the dish of potatoes. Slide the cold shelf on to the second set of runners from the bottom of the roasting oven.

For a three- or four-oven Aga place the shelf on the bottom set of runners of the baking oven and slide in the dish of potatoes.

Bake the dauphinois for 40–50 minutes until the potatoes are soft when pierced with a sharp knife. If you like a golden finish then put the dish towards the top of the roasting oven for 10–15 minutes until golden brown.

Conventional cooking: cook at 180C/350F/Gas mark 4 for 1–1½ hours

Game Chips

Game chips are very thinly sliced potatoes that are deep fried and not roasted. Should you want to serve them with roast game I suggest buying good quality hand-made crisps and heating them briefly in the roasting oven.

Pumpkin and Squash

Pumpkins and squashes have become much more poplar in the last few years. They look so attractive in the autumn but I often wonder if the shoppers know what to do with them! Other than making soup I think the only worthwhile way to cook these vegetables is to roast them for flavour.

You can prepare the pumpkins and squashes in two different ways. One is to peel and cut the flesh into large dice and the other is to half the vegetable and remove the seeds and roast with the skin on. Skin-on looks more interesting but is not so refined!

Here is a recipe for butternut squash. This is the way to roast all other pumpkins and squashes.

Cut the butternut squash in half lengthways and remove the seeds and pith with a spoon. Cut each half into halves or quarters again, depending upon the size of the squash. Lay the squash portions on a baking tray. Melt together some butter and olive oil and brush the cut edges of the squash with the buttery oil mixture. Sprinkle a little salt and pepper over the squash. If you like one or two sprigs of thyme can be tucked around the pieces of squash.

Hang the baking tray on the second set of runners from the bottom of the roasting oven and roast for 25–30 minutes. If you like more colour on the roast squash put the baking tray one runner higher. The flesh should be tender and slightly tinged with colour.

Summer Vegetables

Roast summer vegetables are so versatile. They can be eaten hot straight from the oven, cooled and tossed in salad dressing or as part of a vegetable lasagne or pasta sauce.

The choice of vegetables can be dictated by what is to hand or personal taste. In the summer you may find that you have a glut of one or two particular vegetables – courgettes or tomatoes perhaps – so the vegetables listed below are just a suggestion.

1 red onion, peeled and quartered
1 aubergine, trimmed and cut into chunks
2 courgettes, trimmed and thickly sliced
1 red pepper, seeded and cut into chunks
2–3 tablespoons olive oil
Salt and pepper

Place the vegetables on a shallow baking tray lined with Bake-O-Glide. Drizzle over the olive oil and toss the vegetables in it. Lightly season with salt and pepper.

Hang the tray on the second set of runners from the top of the roasting oven and cook the vegetables for 20 minutes. Check the vegetables and if you like them a little charred return the tray to the oven for 10 minutes longer.

Serve hot or cold as a salad.

Sweet Potatoes

Sweet potatoes have become much more readily available over the last few years and make a good addition to the roast vegetable selection. I often roast them with the roast potatoes.

Peel the sweet potatoes and cut into portions. Toss in a little fat or oil and lay on a baking tray lined with Bake-O-Glide. Hang the tray on the second set of runners from the top of the roasting oven for 20–30 minutes. Move to the floor of the oven for a further 20 minutes until tingeing with colour and soft.

Serve immediately.

Tomatoes

Roasting or baking tomatoes in the oven drives off some of their liquid and intensifies their flavour. They can be served as a simple accompaniment to fish or lamb or they can be used to add an intense flavour to soups and salads.

I find that hothouse grown tomatoes contain a lot of water and will take longer to roast, but roasting will improve their flavour. As with all things buy the best quality that you can afford.

Tomatoes
Olive oil
Sea salt

Cut each tomato in half through the circumference. Lay the tomatoes, cut side uppermost on a baking tray lined with Bake-O-Glide. Drizzle over a little olive oil and sprinkle with a few flakes of sea salt.

Hang the tray on the third set of runners from the top of the roasting oven and roast the tomatoes for 40–50 minutes, depending upon their water content. The tomatoes should be wrinkly and tinged with colour.

Conventional cooking: Most of the above will be cooked in the same oven as roasting meat. However if you wish to cook them separately then set the oven to 200C/400F/Gas mark 6

Vegetables

Accompaniments

Who could think of roast beef without Yorkshire puddings coming to mind? Or lamb without mint sauce? Which bird or loin isn't made complete without stuffing? Here are a wealth of suggestions which cross the 't' on the word roast.

Stuffings, Yorkshire puddings, Gravies and Sauces

Stuffing

Stuffing has traditionally been used to flavour and keep meat moist. It is now frequently cooked as an accompaniment to the roast joint and can be used to make the meat stretch a little further.

The cavity of birds was traditionally stuffed but nowadays we are advised only to stuff the neck end and leave the cavity free so that the bird is thoroughly cooked.

Stuffing can also be used when a joint has been boned and the stuffing fills the bone cavity.

In this section, I have given a variety of stuffings. We have traditional flavours for different meats but they can be interchanged to add variety to your meals.

Homemade stuffing is a million miles away from the packet variety in flavour so if you are always in a hurry keep some breadcrumbs handy in the freezer to make some stuffing. The remaining ingredients don't take long to prepare.

Yorkshire puddings

How many times am I told during Aga cookery demonstrations that the Aga is no good for making Yorkshire puddings and another oven has to be used! The problem being that the Aga oven will not be hot enough to make good Yorkshire puddings after cooking a roast. Well that's certainly true, so the trick is to make your puddings *before* cooking your roast. It should guarantee you perfect results, so do please try the recipe that follows.

Gravy and sauces

A good gravy or sauce is essential with roast meat and yet I meet so many people who cannot make gravy! It isn't difficult to make and I don't add any fancy ingredients as the flavour from the pan juices should be enough. When I was training at college we were always taught to make thin pale gravy for light meats such as pork and chicken and a thick dark gravy for meat such as beef and lamb. My family however, seem to like plenty of thick, dark and flavoursome gravy. Make the gravy to the thickness you like. Putting an onion underneath the roasting meat will guarantee a rich colour and flavour.

Sage and Onion Stuffing

A traditional stuffing for turkey, chicken and goose.

15g/¼ oz butter
1 large onion, peeled and finely chopped
1kg/2¼lbs good quality sausagemeat
225g/8oz streaky bacon, rind
*   removed and finely chopped*
1 tablespoon finely chopped sage
Salt and pepper

Heat the butter in a frying pan and sauté until soft but not brown. Cool. Put the sausagemeat in a bowl and add the diced bacon. Work together well, using the hands is easiest. Season with salt and pepper and then add the onion and the sage. Mix very well.
    Use this stuffing to stuff the neck end of a bird or to form into stuffing balls.

Parsley and Lemon Stuffing

This is a lovely fresh tasting stuffing for turkey or chicken. I like this to stuff the neck end of the bird and then I put a whole lemon in the cavity to add additional flavour. If you replace the lemon rind with chopped sage this stuffing is excellent with roast duck.

25g/1 oz butter
2 onions, peeled and finely chopped
2 sticks of celery, finely chopped
225g/8oz fresh breadcrumbs
4 tablespoons finely chopped parsley
Finely grated rind 2 lemons
Salt and pepper
1 egg, beaten

Melt the butter in a roomy saucepan and add the chopped onion and celery. Toss in the butter and cook slowly until soft but not browned. Remove from the heat and stir in the breadcrumbs, parsley and lemon rind. Mix well and season with salt and pepper. Stir in the beaten egg to bind the stuffing together.
    Use some of the stuffing to stuff the neck cavity and cook any left as stuffing balls.

Apple and Prune Stuffing

Goose is traditionally eaten in the autumn when home grown apples come into season. The fruits add a delicious moistness to this stuffing.

15g/½ oz butter
1 onion, peeled and finely chopped
225g/8 oz ready-to-eat prunes
1 large cooking apple, peeled, cored and
*   very finely chopped*
4 tablespoons port
1 tablespoon finely chopped sage
110g/4 oz fresh breadcrumbs

Melt the butter in a frying pan and add the onion. Cook until softened but not brown. If you have the giblets from the goose chop the liver and add to the onion and cook for 2–3 minutes.

Remove the stones from the prunes and chop the flesh. Stir the prunes and the port into the onions along with the apples. Cook for 4–5 minutes and then remove the pan from the heat. Stir in the sage and the breadcrumbs and season with salt and pepper.

Use the stuffing to stuff the neck end of a 4–5kg/9–11lb goose.

Apricot Stuffing

Dried apricots are a constant standby ingredient in my store cupboard, useful in so many ways. In a stuffing they add juiciness as well as a tang. I have used this stuffing with all meats except beef and venison. This stuffing is easiest made in a blender otherwise chop the ingredients finely.

75g/3oz butter
75g/3oz dried apricots, ready-to-eat or soaked
1 onion, peeled and quartered
75g/3oz walnuts
Finely grated rind and juice 1 orange
150g/5½oz fresh breadcrumbs
Salt and pepper

Put the butter in a basin at the back of the Aga until the butter has melted.

Place the remaining ingredients in a blender or processor and whizz until everything is evenly chopped but is not too fine. Pour in the melted butter to bind the stuffing together.

Makes enough to stuff the neck of a turkey or a rolled joint of lamb or pork.

Cranberry and Almond Stuffing

I love this fruity stuffing at Christmas time not just with turkey but with any roast meats.

3 tablespoons caster sugar
3 tablespoons water
110g/4 oz cranberries
110g/4 oz fresh breadcrumbs
A small onion, peeled and finely chopped
50g/2oz blanched whole almonds,
*   cut in half lengthways*
Finely grated rind ½ lemon
Salt and pepper

Put the caster sugar and water in a saucepan and stand on the simmering plate to dissolve the sugar. Pick over the cranberries, removing any that are soft. Remove any stalks and add them to the sugar syrup. Cover the pan and cook the cranberries until the skins pop, about 4–5 minutes. Remove from the heat.

Put all the remaining ingredients into a basin and add the pan contents. Mix well together. If cooking the meat immediately then add the warm stuffing, alternatively allow the stuffing to cool before using.

Enough to stuff the neck cavity of a turkey or large chicken.

Wild Rice Stuffing

I like this stuffing for poussin which takes little cooking. Remove the breast bones and fill the cavity with the stuffing. The birds will look attractive and are easy to eat, even if they take some preparation time.

50g/2 oz butter
2 medium onions, peeled and finely chopped
2 stalks of celery, very finely chopped
2 small carrots, finely chopped
1 bay leaf
A sprig of thyme
400g/14 oz wild rice
400ml/¾ pint chicken stock
Salt and pepper

Enough for 8 poussin

Melt the butter in a saucepan and add the onion, celery and carrots. Cook gently until soft but not browning, about 5–8 minutes. Stir in the bay leaf, thyme and the rice. Stir to coat the rice with the butter and then add the stock. Cover with a lid and bring the mixture to the boil. Move the pan to the simmering oven for 25–30 minutes. Remove the pan from the oven and fluff up the rice with a fork, draining off any liquid from the cooked rice. Adjust the seasoning and tip the stuffing into a bowl and cool.

Conventional cooking: Cook the rice on the hob in the usual way.

Yorkshire Puddings

Whilst I agree with many that the Aga oven will not be hot enough to make good Yorkshire puddings after cooking a roast, it takes only a little lateral thinking to easily achieve successful results. Make the Yorkshire puddings before roasting the meat and simply re-heat at serving time. I can't tell the difference! I even keep some individual Yorkshire puddings in the freezer for last-minute meals. Yorkshire puddings can be flavoured with chopped thyme or horseradish sauce to ring the changes.

Beef dripping, goose fat or sunflower oil
225g/8oz plain flour
Pinch of salt
2 eggs
Approximately 300ml/½ pint milk

Makes 12 individual Yorkshire the puddings.

I use a 12-hole deep muffin tin to make 12 individual puddings. The heat from the sides of the deep tins helps the puddings to rise.

Put a little dripping or fat or 1 teaspoon oil in each tin. Put the tray directly on the floor of the roasting oven.

Make the batter. Put the flour and salt in a mixing bowl. Add the eggs and a little milk. Start whisking the liquids into the flour gradually adding more milk to make a smooth batter, the consistency of double cream (before whipping).

By this time the fat should be smoking hot. Remove the muffin tray from the oven and ladle in the batter. Hang the shelf on the third set of runners from the top of the roasting oven and slide in the tray of Yorkshire puddings. Cook the puddings for 35–40 minutes until the puddings are risen and golden brown. Some Agas cook more on one side than the other and you may need to turn tray round half way through cooking.

Remove the cooked Yorkshire puddings from the oven and either serve immediately or leave to rest until needed. When needed return to the oven for 8–10 minutes to heat through.

Conventional cooking: Pre-heat the oven to 220C/200C Fan/425F/Gas mark 7. Heat the tin with the fat in until smoking, about 10 minutes. Pour in the batter and cook the Yorkshire puddings for 25–30 minutes until risen and golden.

Smooth Gravy

For smooth gravy equip yourself with a balloon whisk and a flour shaker. Have a jug or gravy boat warming on the back of the Aga ready to receive the hot gravy. Use stock or vegetable water for the liquid and if you like you can deglaze the roasting pan with wine for extra flavour.

Remove the meat from the roasting tin and put on a plate to keep warm. If there is a lot of fat in the pan drain it off and put about 2 tablespoons of fat back in the pan. At this stage pour in a little wine if you like and stand the pan on the simmering plate to bubble and reduce. Remove from the heat. Using the flour shaker sprinkle a thin layer of flour over the roasting tin and using the balloon whisk stir the flour into the fat, scraping up all the sediment as you do so. Repeat with a second or third sprinkling of flour and then gradually whisk in any reserved pan juices, without the fat, and some stock. Put the roasting tin on the simmering plate and continue to whisk while the gravy starts to thicken, adding more stock as needed. Give the gravy a fast boil to get piping hot before pouring into a serving jug.

Conventional cooking: Put the roasting tin on a hob and cook as above.

Stock

Stock can be made from leftover carcass bones or from raw bones from the butcher. How many of us have quantities of stock in our freezer that is not used because the portions are too much for gravy or soup? Freeze concentrated stock in ice cube trays or soup size portions.

Put the bones in a saucepan and add some onion, celery, leek or carrots. Add some peppercorns and a little salt. Pour on enough water to barely cover the bones and put on a lid. Stand on the boiling plate and bring to the boil. Move the pan of boiling stock to the simmering oven and leave to cook for 2–3 hours.

Remove the pan from the oven and allow to cool. Skim off any fat. Strain the stock and boil to reduce the quantity if that is more convenient. Cool and refrigerate or pour into containers and freeze.

Conventional cooking: When the stock has been brought to the boil reduce the heat on the hob to a gentle simmer.

White Sauce

A white sauce is the basis for so many dishes such as soufflés. The basic sauce can be flavoured with parsley to go with ham or cheese for fish. Change the milk to stock and a velouté sauce is made.

I find making a sauce by the 'all in one' method more reliably smooth and glossy. Remember to whisk constantly to ensure a smooth and shiny finish.

300ml/½ pint milk
25g/1oz butter
25g/1oz plain flour
Salt and pepper

Put all the ingredients in a non-stick saucepan. Whisk to start mixing in the flour and then stand the pan on the simmering plate. Continue to whisk gently while the milk is heating and the butter melting. As the sauce heats it will become thicker. Continue to cook for 1–2 minutes so the sauce does not have a raw flour flavour.

Remove the pan from the heat and whisk in any flavourings such as parsley or cheese. Adjust seasoning.

Horseradish Sauce

This is the classic sauce for roast beef and is delicious in beef sandwiches. If you can get fresh horseradish it really is worth the effort of making your own.

150ml/5fl oz double cream
1–2 tablespoons grated fresh horseradish, depending upon taste
2 teaspoons white wine vinegar

Lightly whip the cream and fold in the remaining ingredients. Chill for 2–3 hours to allow the flavours to develop and then adjust seasoning. Serve at room temperature.

This will keep for 2 or 3 days in the fridge.

Mint Sauce

I have memories of making this beautifully aromatic sauce for my mother when I was quite small. For safety I always chopped the mint leaves with a pair of scissors in a jug, which works very well.

A good handful of fresh mint
1–2 teaspoons caster sugar
1 tablespoon boiling water
2–3 tablespoons white wine vinegar

Serves 4–6 with roast lamb

Wash the mint and strip off all the leaves. Chop the leaves finely and put in a small basin and add the sugar and then the boiling water. The boiling water dissolves the sugar and helps to retain the bright colour of the mint. Stir well to dissolve the sugar and then add vinegar to taste.

Onion Sauce

This is another sauce often served with lamb. I like it during the winter months if there is no fresh mint available for mint sauce. It also goes well with chicken and fish.

1 large onion, peeled
25g/1oz butter
300ml/½ pint white sauce (see page 127)
1–2 tablespoons cream

Serves 4

Chop the onion and place in a saucepan. Cover with water and bring to the boil. Boil for 2–3 minutes and drain off the water. Return the onion to the saucepan with the butter and stand on the simmering plate. Cover the pan with a lid and cook the onion gently for 2–3 minutes before moving the pan to the simmering oven for 15–20 minutes. The onion should be soft but not brown. Add the cooked onion to the sauce and sieve or blend if you like a smooth sauce. Heat through gently and then stir in the cream. Check the seasoning and serve.

Apple Sauce

A classic accompaniment for pork. Add more lemon if you like a sharp contrasting flavour to the pork but the amount will depend upon the variety of apples you use. Taste as you go.

½kg/1lb cooking apples
2 tablespoons water
Grated rind and juice ½ lemon
25g/1oz butter
Sugar to taste

Enough for 4–6

Peel and core the apples and place in a saucepan with the water and the lemon rind and juice. Cover with a lid and stand on the simmering plate. Cook until the apples are soft or even turn fluffy. Remove from the heat and either beat with a wooden spoon or mash with a potato masher until smooth. Beat in the butter and taste, adding sugar if needed.
    Serve hot with roast pork.

Cumberland Sauce

Cumberland sauce goes well with ham and can be served hot or cold but is also good with cold game and hot venison joints.

150ml/¼ pint red wine or port
4 tablespoons redcurrant jelly
Finely grated rind and juice of 1 orange and 1 lemon
1 shallot, peeled and finely chopped
1 teaspoon mustard
Small pinch ground ginger

Salt and pepper

Serves 4

Put all the ingredients in to a saucepan along with a seasoning of salt and pepper. Stand on the simmering plate and bring slowly to the boil, stirring occasionally. Cover and remove from the heat. Leave to stand for 10 minutes to allow the flavours to infuse.

If serving hot leave unstrained; to serve cold, strain through a sieve.

Mustard Sauce

Mustard sauce is traditionally eaten with ham and mackerel but I also like it with beef. This sauce is based on a white sauce.

1 quantity of basic white sauce (see page 127)
2 teaspoons dry mustard powder
2 teaspoons vinegar

Serves 4–6

Make the sauce in the usual way but before seasoning with salt and pepper blend the mustard powder and vinegar together and add to the sauce. Stir well to mix and then check and adjust the seasoning.

Cold Mustard Sauce

A different kind of mustard sauce, served cold and made from mustard and oil.

4 tablespoons dry mustard powder
4 tablespoons boiling water
½ teaspoon salt
1 tablespoon olive oil
1 tablespoon capers, crushed or
*   1 tablespoon chopped parsley*

Serves 4–6

Measure the mustard into a basin and add the boiling water. Blend to a smooth paste. Add the salt and gradually add the oil. When smooth season with either capers or chopped parsley.

Bread Sauce

A favourite at Christmas with turkey but always good with roast chicken in the winter. Keep a supply of breadcrumbs from leftover stale bread in the freezer ready for making a bread sauce.

1 large onion, peeled
6–8 cloves
1 bay leaf
6 whole peppercorns

600ml/1 pint milk
110g/4oz fresh breadcrumbs
50g/2oz butter, diced
1–2 tablespoons single cream
Salt

Serves 6–8

Stick the cloves into the onion and place in a milk pan. Add the bay leaf and peppercorns and pour in the milk. Stand the pan on the simmering plate and bring the milk slowly to the boil. Remove from the heat and stand at the back of the Aga for 30 minutes to allow the flavours to infuse.

Strain the milk through a sieve and return to the rinsed out pan. Return the pan to the simmering plate and add the breadcrumbs and then the diced butter to the warm milk. Stir well until the butter has melted and the sauce is thickened. Remove from the heat and stir in the cream and season with salt to taste.

Redcurrant Jelly

Redcurrant jelly is a favourite with lamb and it is useful to add to sauces and glazes. You can of course easily buy redcurrant jelly but it is simple to make at home.

1.25kg/2lb 12oz redcurrants, on their stalks
Caster or preserving sugar, see recipe for quantity

Makes about 5–6 jars

Wash the fruit but leave it on the stalks. Put into a large pan and pour on about 850ml/1 ½ pints water. Stand on the boiling plate and bring to the boil. Move to either the simmering plate or simmering oven and cook until the fruit is soft.

Pour the fruit into a jelly bag suspended over a basin and leave to drip overnight. Do not be tempted to squeeze the bag, as any forced liquid will make the jelly cloudy.

Measure the juice into a very large pan or preserving pan and add 450g/1lb sugar for every 600ml/1 pint liquid. Stand on the simmering plate and stir to dissolve the sugar. When completely dissolved move the pan to the boiling plate and bring the jelly to the boil. Boil rapidly until the jelly reaches setting point (when a spoonful on a cold saucer wrinkles when pushed). Be sure to remove the pan from the heat while the test is setting. When setting point has been reached skim off any scum and pour into clean, sterile jars. Cover with wax discs and a lid when either piping hot or completely cold. Label and store.

Cranberry Sauce

Cranberry sauce has now become an essential accompaniment for the Christmas turkey. I like to use it with cold meats and with venison.

250g/9oz cranberries
75g/3oz caster sugar
Grated rind and juice 1 orange

Pick over the cranberries and remove stalks and any bruised and soft berries. Add the sugar and the grated rind and juice of the orange. Cover with a lid and stand the pan on the simmering plate and allow to cook gently. You will probably hear the cranberries popping. When all the cranberries are cooked, after about

5 minutes, remove from the heat. Stir through.

Serve immediately or cool and keep in an airtight container in the fridge for 3 or 4 days. Serve warm or cold.

This will freeze for up to 1 month.

Orange sauce

I know it sounds old hat to serve orange sauce with duck but it really does go very well. Make in the roasting pan while the meat is resting. This sauce also tastes delicious with a roast ham joint.

1 tablespoon flour
Grated rind and juice 2 oranges
2 tablespoons red wine
2 tablespoons redcurrant jelly
50ml/2 fl oz dry sherry
Sliced oranges and watercress to garnish.

Drain the fat from the roasting tin and return 2 tablespoons of the fat for the sauce. Sprinkle over the flour and whisk with a balloon whisk until smooth. Whisk in the rind, juice, redcurrant jelly and sherry. Whisk until smooth and then stand the roasting tin on the simmering plate or hob. Whisk constantly while the jelly melts and the sauce thickens and bubbles. Allow to bubble for 2 minutes and then check the seasoning.

Pour into a warm serving jug and serve with the carved duck and garnished with the orange slices and watercress.

Mayonnaise

This may seem an odd sauce to put in with roasts, but it can be useful with cold meats.

Make sure the eggs do not come straight from the fridge, the mayonnaise will almost certainly curdle if you do. Lemon juice or wine vinegar can be used and if you find all olive oil too heavy use a mixture of olive oil and a lighter salad oil or rapeseed oil.

2 egg yolks
Pinch dry mustard
Salt and pepper
1 tablespoon white wine vinegar or lemon juice
300ml/½ pint olive oil
1–2 tablespoons boiling water

Makes 300ml/½ pint

Place the egg yolks, a seasoning of salt and pepper and the vinegar or lemon juice in a blender. Whizz together. Pour the oil into a jug. Have the blender whizzing and slowly pour in the oil in a slow, steady stream. By the time all the oil has been added the mayonnaise should be a thick emulsion. Whizz in the boiling water, this gives a lighter colour and slightly softer consistency.

Makes 300ml/½ pint.

Provencal Breadcrumbs

This is a useful way to use up oddments of bread and herbs from the garden. Make batches and freeze. These crumbs are good for coating meat and fish, making stuffings and mixed with cheese to sprinkle over gratins.

110g/4oz bread
A small bunch of parsley, leaves picked from the stalks
4 sprigs rosemary or thyme, leaves removed
2 cloves garlic, peeled and roughly chopped
2 tablespoons olive oil
Salt and pepper

Put the bread, roughly cut into slices, on a baking tray and pop into the simmering oven. Leave for 3–4 hours until really dried out.

Put the parsley and rosemary or thyme and the garlic in a blender or processor and whizz. Add the dried bread and whizz to crush and make a coarse texture. Add the olive oil and season well.

Use this quantity for the lamb or make in larger batches and freeze.

Leftovers

That wonderful bonus which comes with so many roast meals – the chance of a second equally splendid dish the following day! Here are some suggestions for extending and enjoying your roast beyond a first meal.

Leftovers

So often I read that a roast is an expensive meal and is only justified for high days and holidays. I disagree. As long as all the leftovers are used wisely it can become an economical meal.

On hearing the title of this book, most friends said, 'you are putting in a section on leftovers, I hope?' So here it is: some ways to use those leftovers.

I have given quantities but you may not always have the exact amount of say chicken leftover, in most cases it doesn't matter. You can always bulk out the main ingredient with rice or potatoes or cheese. Hard-boiled eggs are a useful meat or fish extender.

You can also swap the meats or fish given; for example, the risotto recipe with pheasant works well with chicken and fish. Different vegetables with similar textures can also be swapped, for example peas instead of broad beans and Chinese leaves instead of cabbage. Don't be afraid to experiment!

When using leftovers extra flavourings are often needed and a sauce to moisten as pre-cooked meat can be dry. Take care not to overcook meat a second time round but also be aware of re-heating thoroughly.

Any leftover meat should be covered to prevent drying out and refrigerated as soon as possible. Gravy and sauces should be reheated to boiling point when serving hot for the second time.

Brussels Sprout Gratinée with Stilton Crust

If your family only like one or two sprouts at a time with their Christmas meal you may be left with cooked sprouts. This is a good way to use up leftover sprouts and some bits of Stilton as well.

*About 700g/1½lbs cooked
    Brussels sprouts
150ml/¼ pint double cream
1 egg
Grated nutmeg, about a ¼
    of a nut*

*75g/3oz Stilton
75g/3oz fresh breadcrumbs
½ teaspoon cayenne
    pepper
Salt and pepper*

Serves 4–6

Put the Brussels sprouts in a food processor and add the egg and nutmeg. Whizz until fairly smooth. Season with salt and pepper and pour into an ovenproof dish.

Crumble the Stilton into a bowl and add the breadcrumbs and cayenne pepper. Stir to mix together and then scatter over the Brussels sprout mixture.

Stand the dish in a roasting tin and pour round a kettle full of boiling water. Hang the tin on the bottom set of runners of the roasting oven and cook for 30–40 minutes, until the filling is set and the top crispy.

Serve with a leafy salad.

Conventional cooking: Pre-heat the oven to 180C/350F/Gas mark4.

Cook's note
If you don't have a food processor the sprouts can be chopped finely with a knife on a board, an easy job as they are cooked and fairly soft.

Bubble and Squeak Cake

Use up leftover roasted Brussels sprouts or cabbage and mashed potatoes in this dish. Serve with good sausages and an onion chutney or perhaps slices of cold roast ham.

175g/6oz onions, peeled and finely chopped
175g/6oz cooked Brussels sprouts or cabbage, chopped

2 tablespoons vegetable oil
700g/1½lbs cold mashed potatoes
Salt, pepper and a grating of nutmeg

Serves 4

Heat the oil in a frying pan and add the onions. Stir well and put on the floor of the roasting oven until golden. After about 10 minutes add the Brussels sprouts and return to the oven for 5 minutes.

Put the potatoes in a mixing bowl and add the cooked onions and sprouts. Add a seasoning of salt, pepper and a grating of nutmeg. Mix all together.

Return the mixture to the frying pan and press down to make a cake. Return the pan to the floor of the oven for 5–6 minutes. Slide the cake onto a plate and then invert into the pan to brown the second side. Cook for a further 5–6 minutes until firm and golden.

Slide the cake onto a warm plate and cut into triangles to serve with the sausages and chutney.

Conventional cooking: Cook in a frying pan on the hob.

Cook's note
This mixture can be made into 8 individual cakes before the final cooking stage.

Chicken and Roast Vegetable Lasagne

Lasagne doesn't have to be made with a traditional meat sauce. Here I use roast vegetables and adding pieces of cooked roast chicken. If you don't have a lot of chicken left over then add some ricotta or mozzarella cheese to bulk it out.

350g/12oz cooked chicken meat, cut into even pieces
1kg/2lb4oz mixed vegetables, onions, courgettes, aubergines, peppers, mushrooms, garlic
2 tablespoons olive oil
Salt and pepper
1 x 400g can chopped tomatoes

6 torn basil leaves
350g/12oz lasagne sheets

For the sauce
50g/2oz butter
50g/2oz flour
600ml/1 pint milk
Salt and pepper
50g/2oz grated Parmesan cheese

Serves 6

Prepare the vegetables in the usual way eg. onions peeled and cut into eighths, peppers seeded and sliced, aubergines cut into chunks.

Lay the vegetables on a baking tray and drizzle with the olive oil. Season with salt and pepper. Hang the tray on the second set of runners of the roasting oven for 20–25 minutes, until the vegetables are cooked and tinged with colour. Stir in the canned tomatoes and the basil. Return to the oven for 10–15 minutes.

Meanwhile make the sauce. Put the butter, flour and milk in a saucepan and whisk together. Stand on the simmering plate and whisk until the sauce thickens and is glossy. Bubble for 2–3 minutes and then remove from the heat. Season with salt and pepper.

Butter an ovenproof dish. Ladle in enough sauce to cover the base. Lay on a single layer of lasagne sheets. Spoon over half the vegetable mixture and half of the cooked chicken. Ladle over some sauce. Repeat with the remaining vegetables and chicken. Finish off with a layer of lasagne and then pour over a final layer of sauce. Sprinkle over the grated cheese.

For a two-oven Aga hang the shelf on the bottom set of runners of the roasting oven. Put in the lasagne and cook for 30 minutes, until bubbling well and golden brown on top. For a three- or four-oven Aga hang the shelf on the second set of runners from the bottom of the baking oven. Slide in the dish of lasagne and bake for 30–40 minutes until bubbling well and golden brown.

Conventional cooking: Roast the vegetables and cook the lasagne at 180C/350F/Gas mark 4.

Cook's note
As this is a re-heated dish as far as the chicken is concerned cook through as soon as the dish is made and do not re-heat any leftovers.

Ham and Olive Lasagne

Lasagne is such a good way of using up leftovers and is especially useful if there isn't all that much meat or fish leftover. If you are not going to cook the lasagne immediately after assembling make sure the sauce is cold before adding the leftover ham. I have listed ham slices but being realistic leftover ham is often in shreds or chunks, so use whatever you have left.

250g/9oz lasagne sheets
1 tablespoon olive oil
1 small onion, peeled and finely chopped
1 clove garlic, peeled
2 x 400g cans chopped tomato
Salt and pepper

About 8 slices of ham, sliced as thinly as possible.
About 8 pitted black olives, halved
2 eggs
150g pot of plain yoghurt
110g/4oz grated Cheddar cheese

Serves 4

Pour the olive oil into a saucepan and add the onion. Stand on the simmering plate and sauté until soft but not browning. Add the garlic and cook for 1 minute. Add the canned tomatoes and allow to bubble. Move the uncovered saucepan to the simmering oven for 15 minutes. Season to taste.

Pour a little sauce into the bottom of an ovenproof dish and place on a layer of lasagne. Pour over the sauce and scatter over the olives. Put in the slices or pieces of ham and top with another layer of lasagne.

In a basin beat the eggs and the yoghurt together, season with salt and pepper and beat in half the grated cheese. Pour the egg mixture over the lasagne. Scatter over the remaining cheese.

For a two-oven Aga hang the shelf on the bottom set of runners of the roasting oven and put in the lasagne. Bake for 30 minutes.

For a three- or four-oven Aga hang the shelf on the bottom set of runners of the baking oven and bake for 40–50 minutes.

The lasagne will be cooked when the lasagne is soft when a knife is inserted in the middle and the topping is set and golden brown.

Conventional cooking: Make the tomato sauce on a hob. Cook the finished lasagne at 180C/350F/Gas mark 4.

Cook's note
This recipe works well with leftover fish such as salmon or trout. To make the lasagne softer put it in a basin and cover with hot water for 5 minutes before draining and using.

Ham and Bean Soup

Leftover ham lends itself very well to soup. If the joint has been boiled and isn't too salty the cooking stock can be used in the soup, but remember this when seasoning the soup. The use of beans in this soup will counteract a lot of the saltiness.

25g/1oz butter
1 onion, peeled and finely chopped
2 celery stalks, diced
2 carrots, peeled and diced
2 tablespoons dry sherry or white wine

2 x 400g cans haricot beans, rinsed
1.2 litres/2 pints ham or vegetable stock
110g/4oz frozen peas
250g/9oz ham, shredded
Roughly chopped parsley or mint to garnish

Serves 6

In a roomy saucepan melt the butter and add the onion, celery and carrot. Sauté on the simmering plate until soft but not coloured. When the vegetables are cooked add the sherry or wine and stir until the liquid had evaporated.

Add half the haricot beans to the pan and mash down with a potato masher and then stir in the stock. Add the remaining beans and bring to the boil. Move to the simmering oven for 10–15 minutes.

Return the soup to the simmering plate and add the peas and the ham. Heat through until the peas are just cooked and the ham heated through.

Ladle the soup into warmed serving bowls and sprinkle over a little chopped parsley or mint.

Serve with bread.

Conventional cooking: Cook this soup on the hob.

Cook's note
Take care not to overcook the ham otherwise it will be tasteless and stringy.

Filled Pancakes

Pancakes make a wonderful casing for all sorts of fillings both sweet and savoury. If you are organised make a good stack of pancakes, interleaved with greaseproof paper, and keep in the freezer. Leftover meat and fish can be combined with a sauce and wrapped quickly in a pancake and popped in the oven.

For the pancakes
110g/4oz plain flour
Pinch salt
1 egg
300ml/½ pint milk

For the filling
25g/1oz plain flour
25g/1oz butter
300ml/½ pint milk
1 tablespoon chopped
   parsley

350g/12oz cooked chicken,
   roughly diced
225g/8oz cooked broccoli
   spears
225g/8oz carrots, diced and
   cooked
75g/3oz grated hard cheese
   e.g. Cheddar, red
   Leicester

Serves 4

Make the pancakes. Place the flour, salt and egg in a mixing bowl. Gradually beat in the milk using a balloon whisk. Add the milk slowly to make a smooth batter. Add enough milk to make the batter the thickness of thick pouring cream.

Heat a large solid-based frying pan on the boiling plate. Pour in a little oil and wipe it round with a wad of kitchen paper. Pour in 2–3 tablespoons or a ladle full of batter and swirl round the pan. Cook for about a minute until the edge is starting to brown. Loosen the pancake with a palette knife and toss the pancake over and cook the second side. Cook for 1–2 minutes until the second side is speckled brown. Slide onto a plate. Continue with the remaining batter to make 8–12 pancakes depending upon the size of your pan.

Cook's note
Cooked chicken, ham, fish or turkey can be used in this recipe.

Make the filling. Put the flour, butter and milk in a saucepan and stand on the simmering plate. Whisk continuously until a smooth sauce has been made. Season with salt and pepper and whisk in the parsley. Remove the pan from the heat and gently stir in the cooked chicken and the vegetables.

Divide the filling between the pancakes and roll up. Lay in an oblong ovenproof dish. Scatter over the grated cheese.

Hang the shelf on the bottom set of runners of the roasting oven and slide in the dish for 20–25 minutes, until the cheese is melted and the filling is piping hot.

Conventional cooking: Heat the pancakes through in the oven set at 180C/350F/Gas mark 4.

Chicken Biriyani

This curry is a useful dish to use up leftovers. I have used chicken for this recipe but it is easily adapted use turkey or pork or even lamb.

2 tablespoons sunflower oil
3 onions, peeled and sliced
50g/2oz cashew nuts
25g/1oz raisins
2 tablespoons masala curry
    paste
400g–500g/14oz–1lb 2oz
    cooked chicken, cubed
1 x 400g can chopped
    tomatoes

250g/9oz good quality
    basmati rice
3 cardamom pods, lightly
    crushed
1 cinnamon stick
6 peppercorns
3 cloves
salt
Pinch saffron strands
    soaked in hot water

Serves 6

Heat 1 tablespoon of oil in a casserole dish and add 2 sliced onions. Stand on the simmering plate and allow to cook until soft but not coloured. Stir in the curry paste and cook for a further 5 minutes. Stir in the cubed chicken and stir to coat in the curry mix. Stir in the chopped tomatoes and cover with a lid. When the mixture is starting to bubble move to the simmering oven for 20–30 minutes.

Measure the rice into a measuring jug and then pour into a saucepan. Pour on 1½ times the volume of the rice in water into the pan with a seasoning of salt, the cardamom pods, cinnamon, peppercorns and cloves. Cover, bring to the boil and move to the simmering oven and cook for 15 minutes, until the rice is cooked and has absorbed all the water.

Meanwhile heat the remaining tablespoon of oil in a frying pan and fry the remaining onion slices until they start to brown. Add the cashew nuts, stir well and cook for 1–2 minutes and then stir in the raisins. Set aside.

Serve the rice and chicken mixture layered on warm plates and the onion mixture scattered on the top.

Conventional cooking: This can be made entirely on the hob or the meat can be heated in a pre-heated oven at 200C/400/Gas mark 6.

Cook's note
Any type of curry paste can be used you that you may have to hand.

Lamb and Tomato Bake

Shepherds' pie is the traditional way to use up leftover lamb but this alternative works really well and is a firm family favourite.

500g/1lb 2oz cooked lamb,
  finely chopped or minced
2 x 400g cans chopped
  tomatoes
1 sprig of rosemary
6 black olives, stoned and
  roughly chopped
25g/1oz pine nuts
Salt and pepper

4 large tomatoes, thinly
  sliced

For the topping
150g/5 ½oz Greek yoghurt
1 egg, beaten
25g/1oz grated Parmesan

Serves 4

Put the prepared lamb in a saucepan, add the tomatoes and sprig of rosemary. Place on the simmering plate and bring to a bubble, cover and move to the simmering oven for half an hour.

When the lamb is piping hot remove from the oven. Pull out the sprig of rosemary and stir in the olives and pine nuts. Season with salt and pepper.

Lay some sliced tomatoes in the base of an ovenproof dish. Spoon in the lamb mixture. Lay on the remaining tomato slices.

In a basin mix together the egg and yoghurt. Season with salt and pepper. Spoon over the layer of tomatoes. Scatter over the grated Parmesan.

Hang the shelf on the bottom set of runners of the roasting oven and slide in the lamb and tomato bake. Bake until the topping has set, is golden brown and the meat is piping hot, about 30 minutes.

Conventional cooking: Cook the lamb on the hob until hot and thick. Bake in the oven pre-heated to 190C/375F/Gas mark 5.

Cook's note
The quantity of lamb will vary according to the amount you have leftover. If the quantity of lamb is not enough stir in some roughly diced feta cheese when spooning in to the dish.

Risotto

A favourite of mine for its sheer versatility. As well as using the leftover meat if you have some cabbage or sprouts left then shred finely and put these in at the end. It really is worth spending time to stir well during the making to give a lovely creamy dish. Making risotto is a great stress-reliever!

Cold pheasant or other bird
25g/1oz butter
1 onion, peeled and
    chopped
250g/ 9oz Arborio rice
1 wine glass of white wine,
    optional
1 litre/1¾ pints hot chicken
    or vegetable stock

Grated rind and juice
    1 lemon
50g/2oz frozen peas
1 tablespoon chopped
    parsley

Serves 4

Cut the cold meat into thin slivers and set aside.

Heat the butter in a roomy sauté pan and add the onion. Cook until soft but take care not to let it colour. Stir in the rice and stir to coat with the onion and butter mixture. Pour in the wine if using, and allow to bubble away. Stir in the hot stock a ladle full at a time. Stir frequently while gradually adding the stock. Allow the stock to be absorbed by the rice before adding more.

When nearly all the stock has been absorbed add the rind and most of the juice of the lemon. Add the peas and the slivered meat with the last addition of stock. Stir while heating through and the rice is cooking. Taste some rice to see that it is cooked and stir in the chopped parsley.

The risotto will be creamy if you have stirred it well.

Conventional cooking: Make on the hob.

Cook's note
Always buy good quality risotto rice for best results.

Pork and Apple Pie

Cold pork is not a favourite in my house so I became a little inventive after a photo shoot some time ago when there was a lot of pork leftover and it couldn't possibly be thrown away. This is now a firm favourite in the Walker household!

Cold pork slices, enough to three-quarter fill a pie dish
2 apples, cored and cut into thick slices or leftover roast apples

Gravy, if any left from the roast or 300ml/½ pint chicken stock
300g/10.5oz puff pastry
1 egg, beaten, to glaze

Serves 4–6

Cut the pork into bite-sized pieces and put in a pie dish. Pop the apple slices between the layers of meat. Pour over the gravy or stock.

Roll the pastry to fit the top of the pie dish. Cut the pastry to shape and use any trimmings to put round the edge of the pie dish. Dampen the pastry and lay over the rolled piece cut to fit. Knock up the edges and flute. Pierce a small hole in the middle. Brush the pastry with the beaten egg.

Hang the oven shelf on the bottom set of runners of the roasting oven, put in the pie and bake for 25 minutes until golden brown, the pastry is puffed and the filling piping hot.

Conventional cooking: Cook the pie at 220C/425F/Gas mark 7.

Cook's note
The size of pie that you make will depend upon the amount of meat you have left. Any stuffing that you have can also be used help the dish go further.

Toasted Sandwiches

I am always surprised by the number of Aga owners I meet who don't realise that you can make brilliant toasted sandwiches on the Aga. Do away with the toast machine, toasties are much nicer made on the Aga simmering plate. Here are a few suggestions but you can let your imagine loose on fillings that you really like.

Mango and Chicken Toastie

110g/4oz cooked chicken , diced
3 tablespoons crème fraîche
1 teaspoon curry paste

2 tablespoons mango chutney
4 slices granary bread
Butter for spreading

Serves 2

In a basin mix together the crème fraîche, curry paste and mango chutney. Fold in the diced chicken.

Spread the bread slices with butter. Divide the filling between two slices of bread. Spread evenly. Top with the remaining slices of bread and press down well.

Lay a sheet of Bake-O-Glide on the simmering plate and lay on the sandwiches. Put down the lid and toast on the one side and then turn over. By the time the second side is toasted the filling should be hot.

Cut each sandwich in half and serve with salad.

Beef and Tomato Toastie

8 slices brown bread
Butter for spreading
175g/6oz sliced beef

Mustard for spreading
4 sliced tomatoes

Serves 4

Spread the slices of bread with butter. Spread each slice with some mustard, the quantity depending upon taste. Lay on the slices of beef followed by slices of tomatoes. Sandwich the slices together to make 4 sandwiches.

Lay the sandwiches on the simmering plate lined with Bake-O-Glide. Put down the lid and toast for 3–4 minutes or until toasted. Turn over the sandwiches and toast the second side. Toast for 4–5 minutes or until toasted on the second side.

Serve immediately.

Crusty Beef Baguette

75g/3oz butter
4 anchovy fillets
Finely grated zest 1 lemon
8 slices cooked beef

Small bunch watercress,
trimmed and washed
1 baguette, cut into 4

Serves 4

Put the butter, anchovy fillets, lemon zest and a grinding of pepper in a basin and beat together well.

Slice the 4 portions of baguette horizontally. Lay the cut sides down on the simmering plate and toast. When golden brown spread each piece well with the anchovy butter. Lay 2 slices of beef on 4 baquette portions, top with watercress and place a piece of baguette on top to make a sandwich.

Turkey and Stilton Patties

These patties can be made into any size, little ones to serve with drinks or as I prefer with the sauce for a lunch dish.

110g/4oz Stilton
3 tablespoons chopped parsley
110g/4oz fresh breadcrumbs
700g/1½lbs cooked turkey meat
1 tablespoon chopped thyme
4 eggs
2 teaspoons mustard
1 clove garlic, peeled
Salt and pepper

Flour for dusting
Small amount vegetable oil for brushing

For the mushroom sauce
450g/1lb mixed mushrooms, wiped and sliced
50g/2oz butter
300ml/½ pint vermouth or dry white wine
500ml tub crème fraîche
Salad leaves to garnish

Serves 4

Cut the Stilton into small cubes and set aside. Mix the parsley and breadcrumbs together and set aside.

Put the turkey meat in a food processor along with 3 eggs, mustard, garlic and a seasoning of salt and pepper. Process until a paste. Divide the mixture into 12 portions and make each into a flat round. Put a cube of cheese in the middle and bring the turkey mixture round the cheese and shape into a ball.

Dust the patties with a little flour. Beat the remaining egg on a plate and roll and brush the turkey patties with the egg. Finally roll the patties in the herby breadcrumbs. Chill well.

When ready to cook brush the patties with a little oil and place on a baking tray. Hang on the third set of runners from the top of the roasting oven for 15–20 minutes until crispy brown.

Meanwhile make the sauce. Melt the butter in a frying pan and sauté the mushrooms for about 5 minutes. Pour in the vermouth or wine and bubble until the liquid is reduced by half. Stir in the crème fraîche. Bubble and cook for 5–10 minutes until syrupy. Season with salt and pepper.

Serve the patties with the sauce and some salad leaves.

Conventional cooking: Put the patties in a frying pan and fry slowly on the hob, turning to gt an even browning.

Cook's note
These patties will hold together best if chilled well before cooking. For the sauce make sure you use full-fat crème fraîche so that it doesn't 'split' during the bubbling stage.

Turkey with Spicy Couscous

A great way to use up leftover turkey.

1 tablespoon olive oil
3 cloves garlic, peeled and
    finely chopped
5cm/2 inch cube ginger,
    peeled and finely
    chopped
2 small red chillies, seeded
    and finely chopped
150ml/5fl oz dry white
    wine
3 tablespoons honey
About 450g/1lb cooked
    turkey meat

For the spicy couscous
300ml/ ½ pint turkey or
    vegetable stock
200ml/7fl oz orange juice

1 teaspoon paprika
½ teaspoon ground
    cinnamon
½ teaspoon ground cumin
1 teaspoon coriander
2 tablespoons olive oil
400g/14oz couscous
Juice 1 lemon
75g/3oz dates, stoned and
    finely chopped
1 orange peeled and
    chopped
6 salad onions, finely
    chopped
1 tablespoon roughly
    chopped coriander
1 tablespoon roughly
    chopped parsley

Serves 4

Heat the oil in a frying pan that can be used in the oven. Add the garlic, ginger and chopped chillies. Cook for 3–4 minutes, taking care not to let the garlic burn. Add the wine and allow to bubble until reduced by half. Stir in the honey and then cook until the sauce becomes thick enough to coat the back of a spoon. Set aside.

For the couscous, put the stock and orange juice in a saucepan along with the spices and olive oil. Bring to the boil. Put the couscous in a roomy bowl and pour on the boiling stock mixture. Cover with a plate and stand at the back of the Aga for 15 minutes.

When the couscous has absorbed all the liquid, fluff it up with a fork and stir in the lemon juice, dates, orange, salad onions, coriander and parsley. Set aside.

Return the frying pan to the simmering plate and when the liquid starts to bubble again, gently stir in the turkey slices. Turn them to coat with the glaze and place the pan on the floor of the roasting oven and cook until starting to caramelize, about 5 minutes. Turn the turkey pieces and return to the oven for a further 5 minutes.

Divide the couscous between four plates and top with the glazed turkey.

Conventional cooking: Cook on the hob.

Cook's note
Add pine nuts or roughly chopped pistachios if you like some added crunch.

Index

Aga**ROAST**

Index

Other Books by Louise Walker

The Traditional Aga Cookery Book
The Traditional Aga Book of Slow Cooking
The Traditional Aga Party Book
The Traditional Aga Book of Vegetarian Cooking
The Traditional Aga Four Seasons Cookery Book
The Traditional Aga Book of Breads and Cakes
Traditional Aga Christmas
Aga Year
The Classic Rayburn Cookbook
The Classic Rayburn Book of Slow Cooking

All published by Absolute Press

Acknowledgements

What a treat it has been to write a book on 'Roasts'. I love Sunday lunch and that just has to be a roast as far as I am concerned. I remember family gatherings as a child and they usually involved a roast meal. Roast lunch was always the centre of exeat weekends for my children and their friends when at school and now that those days have passed, we have room to entertain 'grown-up' friends. Sunday is not the same without the roast.

So thank you to Louise, Phil, Clare and Richard and all our other friends who have tested so many roasts this year.

Thank you to Brian and Chris Mitchard, my butchers for consistently good meat that is a treat to buy, cook and eat.

As always the team at Absolute Press have been supportive in putting together the idea and the reality in the form of this beautifully presented book.

Last, but by no means least, thank you to my family – the children Hanna, Dominic and Hugo who come home with friends to eat me out of house and home and to my husband Geoff who is constantly involved in recipe tests and yet remains slim. And, yes, he does carve, ever since his course at Simpsons in the Strand some years ago!